MW00872782

NORSE MYTHOLOGY

THE COMPLETE GUIDE (2 BOOKS IN 1)

Discover Origins, Traditions, Myths,
And All the Values of Norse Paganism.
Including Gods, Ragnarok Secrets and
Vikings Battles

- By Johan Lindgren

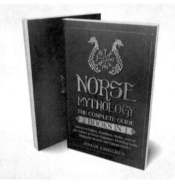

TABLE OF CONTENTS

NORSE MYTHOLOGY

Norse Paganism

INTRODUCTION

Before the Norse (also known as the Vikings) came to Christianity in the Middle Ages, they had their lively native pagan religion as starkly beautiful as the Nordic scenery with which it was closely associated. What we now call "Norse mythology" was at the heart of that religion: a collection of sacred tales that provided meaning to the Vikings' lives. This mythology centered on gods and goddesses like Odin, Thor, Freya, and Loki, interesting and complicated characters.

The Norse religion that comprised these tales was never given a proper name; instead, its adherents called it "tradition." People who continued to follow the old customs when Christianity arrived were dubbed "heathens," a term that originally meant "people who dwell on the heaths" or elsewhere in the countryside, and the term has stayed.

Religions are man's efforts to approach the numinous, and the Norse religion was no different. It gave a method of doing this appropriate for the Vikings' period and location. Even if certain elements of it may strike the contemporary reader as strange, we may recognize the universal human longing to live amid the transcendent beauty and pleasure of the holy if we approach it with the open mind it deserves. Even though it has been a thousand years since the last Vikings lay down their swords, the vibrancy, and wonder of Norse tales and the gods that inhabit them continue to inspire people today.

The Vikings regarded the world to be charmed, in the sense that they didn't feel the need to seek redemption from it, preferring instead to revel in and wonder at "the way things are," which included both "nature" and "culture." Their religions and mythology did not sugarcoat the horror, struggle, and injustice of earthly existence; rather, they accepted it and glorified the endeavor to conquer it via heroic actions for the benefit of oneself and one's people. For the Vikings, "the good life" meant a life filled with such actions.

Many people are acquainted with religious figures and stories from the Norse tribes in modern-day Scandinavia. On the other hand, Norse mythology is more than simply a collection of fascinating people with extraordinary abilities.

Norse mythology is part of an organized and old indigenous religion practiced by the Germanic peoples of Europe, including tribes in central and northern Europe connected by similar languages and religious traditions. Before the Middle Ages, when Christianity became the main religion, this belief system was most prevalent.

Believers utilized Norse mythology myths, like any other religion's stories, to help organize and explain the universe. The gods, living breathing deities who were a fundamental part of existence among the northern Germanic peoples, are the protagonists in those myths.

From the comic book hero Thor to the names of the days of the week, there's something for everyone.

Unlike many of today's major global faiths, the ancient Norse religion was polytheistic, a kind of religious belief in which many gods exist in mythology rather than a single deity. Before their conversion to Christianity, the Germanic tribes worshiped 66 different gods and goddesses.

Odin had ascended to the throne of all gods by the Early Middle Ages. Scholars disagree over when this development took place, and there is a case to be made that Tyr, a god of battle, was initially the gods' leader. In any event, Odin was the heavenly household's head before the conversion of Germanic peoples to Christianity.

Odin is the spouse of Freya, the goddess of fertility and beauty and one of the most animated gods. The deity Loki accuses Freya of indulging in sexual activity with the gods and the elves in one special poem (The Poetic Edda, Lokasenna, stanzas 30 to 32). She denies it, but Loki reminds her that she was discovered in her brother's arms as well. Freya is unable to defend herself against this charge.

Below Odin, there were many more gods, some still well-known today. Thor, for example, was a powerful deity worshipped by all Germanic tribes. He's a devout warrior deity that carries a gigantic war hammer and can summon thunder. On the other hand, Loki is a shady trickster and the father of the half-giantess Hel, the underworld's ruler.

The distinction between Thor and Loki is crucial in understanding how Norse mythology's gods were seen. The gods aren't supposed to be flawless or all-powerful. Instead, they portray real human characteristics, both good and negative.

Norse mythology's gods are simply one of many creatures that live in the universe. In Norse mythology's cosmology or theory of comprehending the structure and order of the cosmos, there are several realms, known as the Nine Worlds, and each one has a distinct species. All nine realms are hanging by Yggdrasil, an ash tree that grows out of the Well of Urd.

Odin — Frigg — Thor — Loki — Tyr
Heimdall — Baldur — Bragi — Idun — Njord
Freya — Freyr — Forseti — Ymir — Mimir

• The human world is known as Midgard. Odin put a fence around it to keep the giants out.

• The kingdom of the giants is Jotunheim.

• Alfheim is where the elves call home.

• Svartalfheim is where the dwarfs call home.

• Asgard is the home of gods and goddesses, especially those of the Aesir people.

• In the Vanir tribe, Vanaheim is the domain of the gods and goddesses.

• Muspelheim is a fire elemental realm.

• Niflheim is an ice-based elemental realm.

• Hel is the underworld and the domain of the dead, ruled by Hel, the half-giantess.

Chapter 1

THE NORSE MYTHOLOGY ORIGINS

Chapter 1: The Norse Mythology Origins

The indigenous pre-Christian religion, attitudes, and stories of the Scandinavian peoples, particularly those who lived in Iceland, where most of the written sources for Norse mythology were compiled, are referred to as Norse mythology.

It represents the best-preserved form of the ancient common Germanic paganism, including Anglo-Saxon mythology.

The Norse Gods are legendary figures from Northern Germanic tribes' traditions from the 9th century A.D. Until the Eddas and other medieval manuscripts were written in the 11th and 18th centuries, these legends were handed down via poetry.

About 50 years after the Prose Edda, the Poetic Edda (also known as the Elder Edda) was committed to writing. It comprises 29 lengthy poems, 11 dedicated to Germanic gods and the remainder to legendary warriors such as Sigurd the Volsung (the Siegfried of the German version Nibelungenlied). Even though it is thought to have been recorded later than the other Eddas, the language and poetic styles used in the stories seem to have been written centuries before their transcription.

Aside from these sources, Scandinavian folklore has surviving tales. Some of them may be backed up by stories found in other Germanic works, such as the story told in the Anglo-Saxon Battle of Finnsburgh and Deor's many references to legendary tales. Scholars can discern the underlying story when multiple incomplete allusions and tellings persist. There are also hundreds more place names throughout Scandinavia named after gods.

The legend is mentioned in a few runic inscriptions, such as the Rök Runestone and the Kvinneby amulet. Several runestones and image stones depict scenes from Norse mythology, including Thor's fishing trip scenes depicting Sigurd (Sigfried), the dragon slayer, Odin, and Sleipnir.

One image stone in Denmark represents Loki with curled dandy-like mustaches and sewn-together lips, while the British Gosforth cross displays various legendary figures. There are also smaller pictures, such as miniatures of Odin (who has one eye), Thor (who wields his hammer), and Freyr (with his enormous phallus).

Humanity was formed from the flesh of Ymir, a primordial entity, and the first two people were named Ask and Embla. The planet will be purportedly reborn after Ragnarok, a war between the Gods and their foes, in which the globe will be engulfed in flames and then born again, fruitful and green, and two people will once again be able to repopulate the earth. The Sun was Sol, a Goddess, the Moon was Mani, a God, and the ground was Joro, another goddess, as in many other ancient societies. Day and night, respectively, were personified as time units by the Viking gods Dagr and Nott.

Sol and Mani are being pursued by the wolves (the sun and the moon)

Norse mythology is preserved in Old Norse dialects, a North Germanic language used in Europe throughout the Middle Ages. These passages were written down from oral tradition in manuscripts in Iceland around the thirteenth century. Poems and Sagas have provided the finest insight into Norse beliefs and deities revered. Objects discovered at pagan burial sites, such as amulets with Thor's hammer and little female figurines regarded as Valkyries, have been interpreted as portraying Norse mythology.

Historians agree that Thor was the most popular god among the Vikings, based on evidence found in documents, place names, and manuscripts. Thor is shown as a courageous protector of humanity, wielding his hammer Mjolnir and destroying Jotnar, gods' and humanity's opponents. Loki is the trickster God, also known as a shapeshifter, responsible for the Gods' and humanity's strife and turmoil. Odin is often referenced in the extant literature, and he is shown as a one-eyed god with a wolf and a raven flanking him as he seeks knowledge throughout the planets.

Odin is also the King of Valhalla, the Viking equivalent of heaven, and is often linked to death. Valhalla, a magnificent and massive hall in Asgard,

was the afterlife for soldiers who died in battle. They would fight all day and then spend their evenings dining, partying, and engaging in general debauchery. Warriors were held in great respect in Norse society.

1.1 Norse Gods

Other gods include Odin's omniscient wife, Frigg, and Freyja, who shares half of the dead with Odin and transports them to Folkvangr, Odin's afterlife realm. Njoror, the God of Ships and Seafaring and Wealth and Prosperity, falls in love with Skaoi, the mountain goddess of hunting and skiing, yet their love is doomed since neither of them can leave their respective homes of the sea and mountains.

The deceased in the Norse afterlife have a variety of places. Hel is an enigmatic kingdom governed by a Goddess of the same name. Valhalla and Folkyangr, as previously noted, were two more possible destinations for individuals who died in the war. The goddess Ran claimed those who perished at sea, while virgins were conveyed by the goddess Gefjon when they died. Reincarnation is commonly mentioned in books explaining stories and Norse mythology, in addition to all of these many endings a soul may reach.

Although Norse Mythology is a complicated belief system with many deities and possible afterlives, the tales and beliefs provide valuable insight into the Norse people. The mythology portrays a warrior and naval society preoccupied with honor via fight and troops who have no fear of death.

1.2 First Giants in Norse Mythology

Lava and sparks poured into the huge vacuum Ginnungagap from Muspelheim in the south. The air from Niflheim and Muspelheim collided in Ginnungagap, the fire melted the ice, but it began to drip, and part of the ice began to assume the form of a humanoid figure. It was a Jötunn, commonly known as a giant, and this giant was Ymir, Norse mythology's first gigantic.

When Ymir went asleep, the perspiration beneath his arms developed two new giants, one male and one female, and one of his legs united with the other to become a third, Thrudgelmir "Strength Yeller." These were the earliest of the jötnar, a family of frost giants. They were nursed by the cow giant Audhumbla, who, like Ymir, was born from Ginnungagap's melting ice.

1.3 Odin Was Born by a Giant

Audhumbla, the enormous cow, ate a chunk of salty ice, and something unexpected occurred while she was doing so. Some human hair sprouted from the block on the first day. Audhumbla licked the salty ice block on the second day, and a head developed.

On the third day, the remainder of the body finally emerged. Buri, the first of the Gods, was the man who had emerged from the salty rock. Buri was a colossus, tall and attractive god. With his wife Bestla, he would have a son named Borr. Odin, Vili, and Ve would be Borr and Bestla's three sons.

1.4 The Death of Ymir

The giants outnumbered the Aesir, which concerned Odin and his two brothers, as did the fact that the giants were continuously conceiving more giants. Because killing Ymir was the only option, the three brothers waited until he was sleeping before attacking him.

A terrifying fight ensued, and they managed to slay Ymir by using all of their might; nevertheless, the blood gushed out of Ymir's corpse with a lethal force in every direction, drowning most of the giants.

Bergelmir and his wife were the only giants to escape; the pair fled to the realm of mist and preserved their lives; all future giants are descended from this marriage.

1.5 The World Was Created

In Norse mythology, the earth was formed from the ashes of the gigantic Ymir. The three brothers brought Ymir's corpse to Ginnungagap's core, where they formed the universe from Ymir's ashes.

Oceans, rivers, and lakes were formed from the blood.

The earth was formed from the flesh.

Mountains sprang out of the bones.

The teeth were turned into boulders.
The hair took on the form of grass and trees.

The eyelashes took on the appearance of Midgard.

They flung the brain into the air, which turned into clouds, as well as the skull into the sky, with Ymir's skull serving as the lid that encased the new planet. The brothers seized some of the sparks flying out of Muspelheim, the region of fire.

They sent the sparks up toward the interior of the skull, which glittered at night and was known as stars. They erected Asgard on the plains of Idavoll, which would be the Gods' dwelling. Giants were permitted to reside in Jotunheim, far away from Asgard.

1.6 The Dwarves Came into Existence

The dwarfs appeared on the scene. Worms began crawling out of the decaying remains of the gigantic Ymir, and these worms would become the dwarves, while Odin and his brothers were in the process of building a new world from the huge Ymir's bodily parts. Because the three brothers Odin, Vili, and Ve were frightened that the sky might tumble down, they enlisted the help of four dwarfs, who were sent in four directions across the globe.

North "Nordi," West "Vestri," South "Sundri," and East "Austri" are the names of the four dwarfs. The remainder of the dwarves chose to live below, among rocks and caverns known as Svartalheim (the Dwarves' Home). They honed their art and developed some of the most powerful and magical weapons, such as Mjölnir, Thor's hammer, as well as gorgeous jewelry.

1.7 The Sun & Moon

Mundilfari, "the one who moves according to certain times" from Midgard, had two offspring who were so gleaming and lovely that he named his son Mani "Moon" and his daughter Sol "Sun."

The Gods were so enraged by their hubris that they kidnapped them and flew them into the sky. Sol would go across the sky in a chariot drawn by two horses named rvakr "Early awake" and Alsvir "Very swift." Svalin, a shield underneath the chariot, shields the soil beneath it from the flames.

Only one horse is used to pull Mani. Aldsvider Mani kidnapped two youngsters from Midgard, Bil, and Yuki, to assist him in driving his chariot. Two wolves chase them, Sköll "Treachery" and Hati "Hate," who take a little bite out of the Moon each day, but the Moon escapes and heals itself. These two wolves will catch the sun and the moon one day during Ragnarok.

1.8 Day & Night

There is, however, a legend of a giant named Nörvi who had a daughter named Nótt" Night." Dagr "Day" was the son of Nótt's daughter. Nótt and Dagr are both riding in chariots drawn by horses.

Her horse Hrimfaxi "rime mane," pulls Nótt. Dagr is behind her, dragged by his horse Skinfaxi "shining mane." These are reportedly followed by the two wolves, Sköll and Hati, which makes this portion of Norse mythology a little confused since there are various and contradictory sagas regarding this phase.

1.9 The First Humans

Odin and his two brothers, Vili and Vé, took a stroll on the beach one day when they discovered two logs, one from an ash tree and another from an Elm tree.

The first two people were formed when Odin gave the logs spirit or life, Ve gave them movement, thinking, and intellect, and Vili gave them shape, speech, emotions, and the five senses. Ask was given the name of the guy, while Embla was given the lady's name. The Aesir determined that humanity should be housed in Midgard.

NORSE TRADITIONS, WORSHIP, AND SACRIFICE

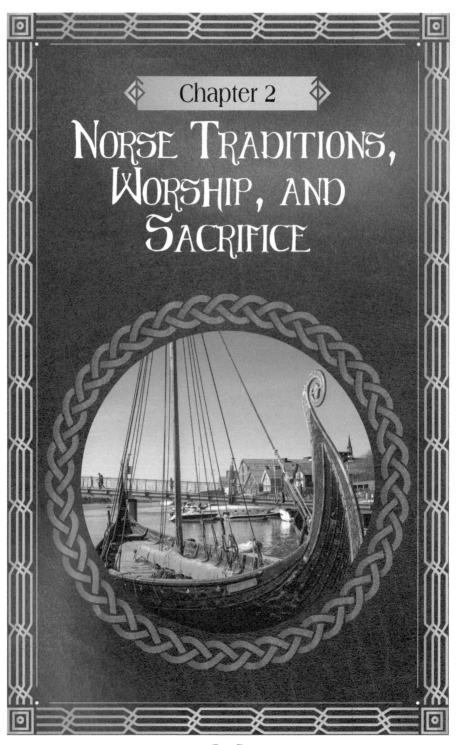

Chapter 2: Norse Traditions, Worship, and Sacrifice

One thousand years after the Viking Age, Thor and Odin are still going strong. Many people believe that with the arrival of Christianity, the ancient Nordic religion—the belief in Norse gods—died out. However, it did not and was instead practiced in secret or behind a Christian shroud. Today, in Denmark, between 500 and 1000 individuals believe in and worship the ancient gods of the old Nordic religion.

A divine (male cult priest). Jonina K. Berg is the photographer.

Like the Vikings, modern adherents of the traditional Nordic religion gather in the open air. They bring sacrifices to the gods and laud them here. They pay homage to the gods by toasting them and feasting on them. To hope for prosperity and a bountiful crop, the toast might be made to the fertility gods Njörd and Frej. Following that, the contemporary believers raise their

glasses in a personal toast. Young ladies, for example, might worship Freyja to get pregnant or discover everlasting love. Thor may be hailed for strength if a hurdle is encountered, while Odin can be summoned for knowledge.

The present belief in Norse gods is not a direct descendant of the Vikings' beliefs. Because there are so few documented records on the topic, it is more of rebirth and reinterpretation of the previous faith. Most of them are short poems written by Christian monks or stories from the sagas.

2.1 What is Asatro?

The worship of the Norse gods is known as "Asatro." Religion includes not just the worship of gods but also giants and ancestors. Asatro is a relatively new phrase that gained popularity in the nineteenth century. When the Vikings discovered Christianity, they didn't have a term for their faith. As a result, they referred to it as "the old way" (Forn Sidr), in contrast to Christianity, which they referred to as "the new way."

Forn Sidr is the name of Denmark's biggest Nordic religious society. It was founded in 1997 and had roughly 600 members. It is Denmark's only legally recognized Nordic religious organization. In 2003, this permission was received. The believers are divided into groups that may be found throughout Denmark. There are also those Christians who want to practice on their own.

Sweden, Norway, and Iceland all have ancient Nordic religious followers. There are also a few groups in the United Kingdom and the United States.

2.2 A Revival of "The Old Way"

Believers in the ancient Nordic religion resurrected the Vikings' beliefs based on tales passed down via written sources, particularly the Elder and

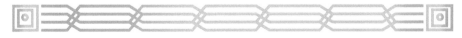

Younger Edda poems. Because there is no one interpretation of the recorded texts, religion is practiced to best suit the person.

Believers in the ancient Nordic religion visit pre-Christian cult sites and make gifts to experience the power of their ancestors. For example, the selected place maybe a Bronze Age burial mound or even a Viking Age ship setting.

A "Gode" (male cult priest) or "Gydje" leads those taking part in the sacrifice (female cult priest). The participants usually form a ceremonial circle. This produces "a sacred area" within the circle—a type of doorway to the gods' realm. After that, the participants reverence their gods until the circle is ceremonially reopened. Depending on the season and the topic of the sacrifice, specific gods are called.

The offerings are made four times a year during the winter solstice, spring equinox, summer solstice, and fall equinox. The winter and summer solstices are the shortest and longest days of the year. The day and night are the same lengths during the spring and fall equinoxes.

2.3 Facts about Asatro

The way the Vikings divided the year was strongly linked to their everyday activities and routines. The sun's annual path and the moon's phases were used to divide the world.

Around the 13th of October, the Viking year started. They began the winter half with a massive public harvest sacrifice. They completed it with a similar victory sacrifice when spring arrived around April 14—the beginning of the warm season. Between these two sacrifices, the Vikings celebrated the winter solstice, the shortest day of the year, on December 21. The days steadily grew brighter and warmer after this day. Like it is now, Christmas was the most important event of the winter portion of the year. The event started in mid-January and continued for several weeks.

The Vikings employed the summer portion of the year to collect supplies. On the year's longest day, known as Midsummer's Eve, the Vikings celebrated their midsummer sacrifice ceremonies, the summer solstice around the 21st of June. After then, the year started to descend into darkness once again. The day and night lengths were once again equal during the fall equinox. The winter part of the year had begun once again, with darkness triumphing over light.

The Viking Age, which began more than 1,000 years ago, was a period of religious transformation in Scandinavia. The narrative is lengthy and complicated, but it is also absolutely intriguing.

Current researchers widely dismiss the image of the early Vikings as pagans who despised Christians. While they may have had pagan ideas, most experts today assume that church assaults were unrelated to religion. To the Vikings, churches and monasteries were poorly fortified structures with valuables hidden behind their walls.

The Vikings were known to worship a variety of gods. This might help to explain why certain people were so willing to accept the idea of a Christian deity.

2.4 The Old Norse Beliefs

Because so little was written down, there isn't much proof of Old Norse paganism. Old Norse, based on rituals and oral tradition, was deeply incorporated into daily life.

So much so that it was mistaken for a way of life rather than a religion. Only Christianity brought the notion of religion as we know it today to Scandinavia.

In Viking sagas, paganism is sometimes referenced. On the other hand, such sagas were largely written down in Iceland in the 13th century, a

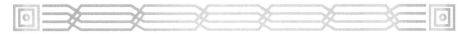

few hundred years after Christianity was established. Who knows how these more current views influenced historical memories?

We know that chieftains served priestly and that pagan rituals most likely included horse sacrifice.

We also know that the Vikings were not a homogeneous group. They lived in small groups throughout a large area. However, it's possible that these tribes viewed themselves as part of a larger Old Norse-speaking community in northern Europe. Many ecological, economic, and cultural links existed between pre-Christian belief systems.

The Vikings, like the Greeks and Romans before them, worshipped several gods. The God of Wisdom, Poetry, and War, Odin, is the most well-known. Other prominent names include Odin's son Thor, the God of Thunder, and the fertility goddesses Freyr and Freyja.

2.5 The Vikings Sailed Far and Wide

The Vikings' invasions on the British Isles elsewhere brought them closer to the Christian world. The Vikings have kept their own beliefs after the attacks but were forced to convert by political pressure if more amicable connections were to be developed.

It was forbidden for Christians to trade with pagans. As a result, many Vikings have had to undergo some type of 'temporary baptism' to trade. It was not a complete baptism, but it demonstrated a desire to embrace Christianity. That was sufficient to enable trading to occur.

2.6 When Christianity Came to Norway

The narrative of Olav Tryggvason returning to Norway with Christianity in tow is well-known. However, the religion had already made inroads into Scandinavia, although limited.

Attempts to convert Scandinavia began as early as the year 725. St Willibrord, an Anglo-Saxon, conducted a mission to Denmark. In the city of Hedeby, Christians and Odin and Thor worshipers coexisted. The Christian cross and Thor's hammer might be purchased at the same jewelry store.

Haakon the Good endeavored to introduce Christianity using his royal power in 950. If he persevered, it became evident that he would lose the backing of pagan chieftains. That sealed his decision, so he dropped the proposal and returned his bishops to the British Isles.

In the summer of 995, Olav Tryggvason returned to Norway to claim the crown. This was the official start of the large-scale conversion.

He took numerous ships, as well as some English clergymen and a bishop, with him. He conducted the first formal Christian mass in Norway when he arrived on the island of Moster. However, it took roughly 35 years for Norway to accept the faith.

According to archaeological evidence, Christianity was progressively accepted. Individual villages might convert or not convert depending on whether or not the local chieftain converted.

2.7 Better Safe Than Sorry

Many people are unaware that the conversion of Norway to Christianity took far longer than they think. We'll never know whether the faiths were considered equivalent or if people just didn't want to disturb the old gods or the new gods.

The intricate carvings on Norway's old stave churches combine Christian and Viking motifs. Many people are surprised by this, given that the oldest surviving specimen dates from the 12th century.

Finely carved gates repeat old legends inside, while many of the church roofs are lined with dragon decorations. Urnes is a UNESCO World Heritage Site and Norway's oldest stave church.

A wonderfully carved artwork on the northern wall depicts a snake biting and bitten by another animal.

The church's Romanesque Basilica layout and the carvings make it a notable example of old Norse symbols combined with medieval Christian influences.

Cemeteries around the U.K., where many Scandinavians settled, bear witness to this long period of transition. The hammer and cross may be seen on certain old gravestones.

Most knowledge regarding the Vikings' beliefs and customs comes from hints found at burial sites or from sagas recorded after their conversion to Christianity. They were pagan, polytheistic, and had a profusion of methods to worship, as Jonny Wilkes investigates for BBC History Revealed.

The Vikings did not have a single organized and institutionalized religion. To begin with, they didn't have a separate social unit, so, understandably, they didn't have a unique set of beliefs and behaviors.

In the Viking Age, paganism differed by location; thus, what people believed in Denmark would differ from what they believed in Norway and Sweden. Each group, and even each household, followed their beliefs in their unique manner. The issue of how they did so is significantly more difficult to answer.

The Vikings' beliefs and rituals were important to them, and they incorporated them into their daily lives. However, there is little evidence to indicate how this would have appeared other than what can be learned from graves and carved images. The sagas and tales that supply most of our knowledge (about Odin, Valhalla, Thor, Ragnarok) were written centuries later and by Christians no less.

Since everything was passed down orally, the Vikings had non-religious scriptures and a few temple-like structures. Natural elements such as trees and rivers, on the other hand, were considered holy and were employed in ceremonies.

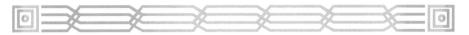

Chieftains and monarchs largely oversaw religious rites and ceremonies. However, evidence implies that völur or seeresses (women with magical and prophetic ability), as well as Godar, existed (heathen priests who functioned as cult leaders).

Priests were most likely the ones who carried out the most important Viking ritual: sacrifice. Although anybody might sacrifice animals or items to the gods, it seems that the Vikings were not opposed to human sacrifices during specific rites, such as funerals.

2.8 Why Were Vikings Buried Inside Ships?

The sea played a significant part in the Vikings' life, and it also played a significant one in their deaths. Vikings were buried with everything they would need for their voyage into the underworld due to their beliefs in the afterlife. Artisans may be buried with their tools, whereas warriors may be buried with their weapons.

A ship burial was the most prevalent method for kings and nobles, and evidence of them has been discovered in Scandinavia, the United Kingdom, and Russia. The deceased were placed on a ship with their belongings and either taken out to sea or buried under a mound. Burial mounds played a secondary use as dynasty territory markers.

The Oseberg ship was discovered in Norway. A full longship, the corpses of two women, as well as horses, clothes, a cart, and chests of merchandise, were discovered.

The Oseberg ship, discovered in the early twentieth century and dated to roughly AD 800, is one of the best-preserved Viking ships ever unearthed. The Viking Ship Museum in Oslo, Norway, presently exhibits.

The Vikings worshipped a pantheon of gods and goddesses who impacted every aspect of their existence and demanded their sacrifices. Women turned to Freya for aid with pregnancy and delivery, while Thor, the thunder god, was rewarded with offerings in exchange for favorable weather. Again, the significance of a deity differed depending on where they were worshipped.

The Vikings believed in gods, Frost, Fire Giants, and a plethora of monsters and animals, including the wolf Fenrir and Jörmungandr, a snake so massive that it ringed Midgard, the human world. The gods lived in Asgard, the giants in Jotunheim, and the deceased lived in Niflheim, cold, gloomy, and foggy. The branches or roots of Yggdrasill, a holy ash tree in the center of the universe, connected the nine worlds in all. Valhalla, a majestic hall in Asgard for those who died in battle, was where all good Viking warriors longed to go. It was thought that they would spend their days perfecting their fighting skills and their evenings sipping the greatest mead and eating on the flesh of an everlasting boa; their wounds miraculously healed. The god Odin welcomed these warriors, knowing that they would fight for him during Ragnarok, the pre-determined end of the worlds when the Sun would darken, the stars

would disappear, the Earth would descend into the sea, and a tremendous battle between gods, giants, and beasts would take place.

2.9 How do we know about Viking mythology with so little evidence?

In addition to several sagas, Icelander Snorri Sturluson's Prose Edda was the most important source for providing a systematic explanation. It covered the mythology from the beginning to the end, from creation to Ragnarok. It was written in the 13th century, long after the Vikings had reached their peak—and therefore after Scandinavia had converted to Christianity; fact, Snorri himself was a Christian—and it contains intriguing insights, but it should not be treated as gospel.

"We can't be certain it hasn't been judiciously reinvented or affected to some measure by Christian theology," argues historian Philip Parker.

The Vikings' understanding of religion would be eternally altered due to their pagan beliefs colliding with Christianity. While the Christians

considered the Vikings heathens and barbarians, the Vikings' choices to attack churches and monasteries were driven by a desire to find undefended valuables.

In reality, according to Parker, they rapidly saw the advantages of Christianity before making the slow conversion: "They had a form of token conversion called primsigning or 'first signing,' where the symbol of the cross was painted on them." It made it acceptable for them to trade.

2.10 When did the Vikings Become Christian?

As the Vikings raided and explored new places, they were more exposed to Christianity. At first, they were eager to accept the trappings of this religion to aid their commerce—after all, what's another deity to add to their pantheon? However, as integration progressed and years passed, a growing number of Vikings converted.

Pagan ideas were often absorbed, resulting in the merging of Ragnarok and Judgement Day. The name of St Peter appears with Thor's hammer on coins discovered in York, for example.

In the case of Scandinavia, politics aided the spread of Christianity. "There were missionaries in the early ninth century, but they didn't make much progress," Philip Parker explains. Instead, kings began converting for political reasons or improving ties with Christian kingdoms, such as Harald Bluetooth of Denmark in roughly AD 960.

Thanks to King Olaf Tryggvason, Christianity had been established throughout Denmark and much of Norway by the mid-11th century.

2.11 Viking Gods

Odin

Odin, the All-Father and king of Asgard, was associated with many things, including battle, knowledge, magic, and poetry. To obtain comprehension of the runes, he gave one of his eyes for the vision of the universe and cosmos and let himself be hung on the world tree, Yggdrasil, for 9 days and nights.

The one-eyed Odin (or Woden, that's where the word "Wednesday" comes from) was sometimes pictured wearing a broad-brimmed hat or cloak to avoid being recognized as he wandered through the human world.

He had two ravens that spied for him and rode an eight-legged horse called Sleipnir. At Ragnarok, Odin would meet his death battling the terrible wolf Fenrir.

Thor

Thor, the god of thunder, lightning, and storms, was one of the most beloved gods in the pantheon since he guarded humanity and Asgard.

With his iron gloves, charmed belt, and, most notably, his mighty hammer, Mjölnir, which could level mountains, the red-bearded son of Odin was capable of fighting giants. In Viking art and culture, his hammer became a universal emblem. We got the word 'Thursday' ('Thor's Day') from his name.

Freyja

Freyr's sister, Freyja was a pleasure-seeking and materialistic goddess linked with love, sex, beauty, riches, and magic. She wore the exquisite Brsingamen necklace and a cape made of falcon feathers that allowed her to fly.

Her name means 'Lady,' and she is one of the few female deities in the Viking pantheon. While the Valkyries chose half of the soldiers killed in battle to join Odin in Valhalla, the other half went to Fólkvangr, a field ruled over by Freyja.

Freyr

Freyr, the son of the sea god Njörd, belonged to the Vanir, one of the two warring races of gods, the other being the Sir. He was the god of fertility and sunlight, prosperity, and peace.

He was one of the most revered gods, particularly in Sweden, and he would accept gifts in exchange for a bountiful crop or virility. Freyr rode a golden boar built by the dwarves and had a ship he could fold into his pocket as well as a sword that fought on its own, according to folklore.

Loki

Loki, the trickster god of mischief (and fire), was a shapeshifter who could take on the forms of animals and humans. However, Loki's antics might be brutal, resulting in the death of a cherished deity.

Freya, Balder's mother, was duped into disclosing her son's single vulnerability, mistletoe, by Loki, who subsequently had the blind god Höd toss a spiked branch of mistletoe at him. Loki joins the giants during Ragnarok but is killed in the fight.

2.12 The Sacrificial Rituals of the Vikings

The Vikings' sacrifice rites included grand festivities in magnate's halls to lake offerings of weapons, jewelry, and equipment. According to documented texts, animals and humans were hanged from trees in sacred groves. Because the Vikings thought that some sacrifice places had especially strong connections with the gods, they utilized them regularly. According to Christian missionaries' testimonies, the Vikings sacrificed to sculptures that stood out in natural settings or in cult structures.

Winter solstice, spring equinox, summer solstice, and autumn equinox are said to have the four fixed blót sacrifices every year. If a problem developed that required the gods' assistance, the Vikings conducted further blót sacrifices.

The Viking town of Hedeby celebrated the winter solstice, according to the Arabic explorer al-Tartuchi. "They have a celebration when everyone comes to honor the deity and eat and drink. The person who slaughters a sacrificed animal erects stakes at his farmyard's entrance and places the sacrificial animal on them. This is so that everyone knows he's sacrificing in the name of his deity." Following the sacrifices, there may be a communal blót feast, in which all of the participants ate and drank together. Animal sacrifices were uncommon and were mostly linked with magnates and monarchs.

2.13 Cult Specialists

Cult experts had an intimate relationship with the gods. Völur, or seeresses, were mentioned in the sagas and archaeological findings. These were ladies who had magical and prophetic abilities. Great persons are known as "Goder," or heathen priests, who served as cult leaders, are also referenced in the sagas and on rune stones. As a result, both men and women may be experts in cultic activities.

The Viking pagan priest Roulv (Hróulfr), also mentioned on other runestones in the southern section of Funen, is mentioned in the runic inscrip

tion on the stone from Helns. The inscription is believed to be from the 700s or 800s. When it was discovered, the stone had fractured into multiple parts, and the highest section was gone. King Frederik VII requested that the runestone be delivered to Copenhagen.

Human sacrifices were practiced throughout the Viking age, according to many stories. Thietmar of Merseburg, a German bishop, recalls how the Vikings gathered at Lejre on Zealand every nine years in January to "give to their gods 99 individuals and exactly as many horses, dogs, chickens, or hawks because these should serve them in the realm of the dead and atone for their wicked actions."

The sacrifice ritual at Gammel Uppsala in Sweden, where the temple was dedicated to Thor, Odin, and Frey, was described similarly by the German monk Adam of Bremen in 1072. Every 9 years, the Vikings gathered here to assure the gods' blessing. In a neighboring sacred wood, 9 males of various living species were sacrificed. Dogs, horses, and people, according to Adam of Bremen, were hanged from the trees. The number 9 had a mystical meaning for the Vikings, and it was used in a variety of ceremonies.

Whether these reports were true or merely Christian propaganda, it has sparked heated discussion. Thietmar and Adam were not present throughout the cult's operations.

As a result, Thietmar and Adam's stories have long been rejected as lies. According to new archaeological discoveries, human sacrifice was a reality in Viking Age Denmark. Skeletons discovered in wells at the Viking fortification of Trelleborg and the magnate's palace at Tiss, both in West Zealand, have caused archaeologists to reconsider their previous assumptions.

2.14 Human Sacrifices at Trelleborg

A sacrifice site was discovered in Trelleborg before constructing the Viking fortification in 980-81. Human and animal remains, jewelry, and ar-

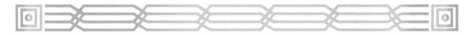

tifacts were discovered in five 3-meter-deep wells. Four of the five human sacrifices were young children ages four to seven.

The fact that the bones were discovered in wells is important. Wells have significant symbolic meaning for the Vikings. Odin's insight came from drinking at Mmir's spring. In return, he had to give Mmir one of his eyeballs. But what might a human sacrifice be repaid with?

A tiny enclosure was discovered near three of the sacrificial wells at Trelleborg. Before the victims were dumped in the deep wells, a sacrifice rite may have been here. Perhaps the sacrifice location was part of the town 300 meters from Trelleborg. The religious site was demolished, and the sacrifices ceased when the fortification was built. Humans were not sacrificed in the emerging Christian faith, gaining popularity.

Chapter 3

THE POEMS OF THE POETIC AND PROSE EDDA

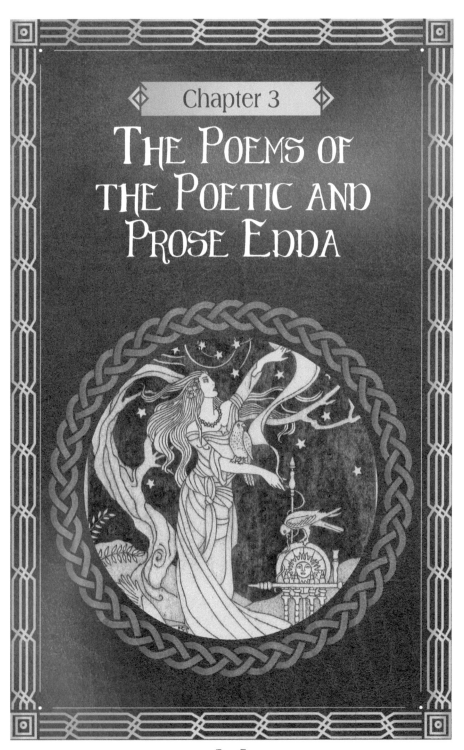

Chapter 3: The Poems of the Poetic and Prose Edda

3.1 Prose Edda

The Prose, or Younger Edda, and the Poetic, or Elder Edda, are two 13th-century texts that comprise a collection of ancient Icelandic literature. It is the most comprehensive and complete source of current Germanic mythological information.

The traditions of Sigurdr and Brynhildr, the Niflungar (treasure-hoarding dwarves), and their successors are mostly told in the Poetic Edda. The Poetic Edda offers poetry about Odin, Freyr, or Thor, followed by heroic lays, beginning with the 'Prophecy of the Sibyl,' which recounts the Norse creation story and foretells the end of the world (narrative epics about heroes).

Snorri Sturluson, an Icelandic chieftain, poet, and historian, wrote the Prose Edda between 1222 and 1223. It is a poetics textbook designed to teach young poets how to write in the challenging meters of the early Icelandic skalds (court poets) and offers a Christian perspective of the legendary topics covered or referred to in early poetry. There is a prologue and three sections to it. Skáldskaparmál ("The Language of Poetry"), which deals with the skalds'

intricate, riddle-like kennings and circumlocutions, and Háttatal ("A Catalog of Metres"), which gives instances of 102 meters known to Snorri, is of primary importance to ancient Norse and Germanic literary experts. The last portion, Gylfaginning ("Gylfi's Beguiling"), is of broad interest to the reader. It is written in the style of a conversation and depicts the visit of Gylfi, a Swedish monarch, to Asgard, the gods' castle. In response to his queries, the gods tell Gylfi Norse mythology about the creation of the universe, the gods' exploits, and the doom that awaits everyone in the Ragnarok (Doom [or Twilight] of the Gods). Dramatic skill, comedy, and charm are used to tell the stories.

The Prose Edda, often known as the Young Edda or Edda of Snorri, is an Icelandic textbook of Scaldic poetry and a Norse mythology anthology. Snorri Sturluson, an Icelandic poet, historian, and statesman, wrote the workaround 1220. It's a must-read for everyone interested in old Norse mythology and poetry.

There are currently seven surviving manuscripts with prose passages from the Edda text, the four most important of which are Codex Upsaliensis (U), the oldest, Codex Wormianus (W), Codex Trajectinus (T), and, above all, Codex Regius (R).

The Uppsala Library in Uppsala, Sweden, houses the Codex Upsaliensis. In prose, the Edda is split into three sections:

• Gylfaginning—Gylfe, a Swedish mythological king, pays a visit to the gods in Aesir and asks them questions about the creation of the world, as well as about the horse Sleipnir.

• Skáldskaparmál—A study of Nordic poetry's metaphorical vocabulary and its mystical connotations, with several allusions to the Edda in verse.

• Háttatal—A poetry collection for scalded poets.

3.2 Poetic Edda

The Poetic Edda is a later manuscript from the second half of the thirteenth century that includes earlier content (hence its alternative title, the Elder Edda). It is a collection of unknown author mythical and heroic poetry written over a lengthy period (AD 800–1100). They are frequently dramatic conversations written in a terse, plain, archaic form that contrasts sharply with the skalds' creative poetry.

Vluspá ("Sibyl's Prophecy"), a broad cosmogonic tale that recounts the history of the gods, humanity, and dwarfs in flashing episodes from the creation of the world to the death of the gods and the destruction of the world, kicks off the mythical cycle.

Hávamál ("Sayings of the High One") follows a collection of disjointed, incomplete, instructional poetry that summarizes Odin's knowledge as a wizard-warrior deity. The commandments are sarcastic and usually amoral, indicating that they were written during a period of lawlessness and betrayal. The bizarre tale of Odin obtaining the magical power of the runes (alphabetical letters) by hanging himself from a tree and enduring hunger and thirst for nine nights is told in the second half. A collection of magical charms concludes the poem.

The amusing Thrymskvida ("Lay of Thrym"), which relates how the giant Thrym takes the thunder god Thor's hammer and demands the goddess Freyja's marriage in exchange for its return, is one of the best mythological poems. Thor disguises himself as a bride and travels to Thrym, where the hilarity stems from the "bride's" astounding manners during the bridal feast when she consumes an ox and eight fish, as well as three jugs of mead.

The Germanic heroes are included in the second part of the Poetic Edda. Except for the Völundarkvida ("Lay of Völundr"; i.e., Wayland the Smith), they are all about the hero Sigurd (Siegfried), describing his boyhood, marriage to Gudrun, death, and the Burgundians' terrible destiny (Nibelungs). These lays are the earliest surviving literary versions of the Germanic mythology of deception, bloodshed, and vengeance at the heart of Nibelungenlied,

the famous medieval German epic. The austere Eddic poems, unlike the Nibelungenlied, which stands on the verge of romance, linger on terrible and violent actions with a bleak stoicism that is unaffected by any civilizing influences.

Poetic Edda or Edda in Verse is a collection of Old Norse poetry preserved in the Codex Regius, a medieval Icelandic book from the 13th century. The book includes 11 mythical poetries and 19 poems by Nordic and Germanic heroes, with the names of the heroes remaining unknown. It is the most significant source of knowledge regarding Norse mythology and legendary Germanic heroes, alongside Snorri Sturluson's prose Edda.

This work is a compilation of old poetry about gods and heroes from the past, vestiges of oral heritage. It contains stories concerning the creation and destruction of the universe, tales of asses (Aesir) gods such as Odin, Thor, and Frey, and heroes such as Siegfried. The following are the major poems:

- Völuspá (Prophecy of the Wise Woman, Prophecy of the Seer)

- Hávamál (The Highest Ballad, Hár's Sayings, Hár's Sayings)

- Vafrnismál (The Ballad of Vafthrdnir, The Song of Vafthrdnir, Vafthrdnir's Sayings)

- Grmnismál (The Grmnir Ballad, The Grmnir Song, and The Grmnir Sayings)

- Skrnismál (The Skrnir Ballad, The Skrnir Song, and The Skrnir Journey)

- Hárbarsljó (Hárbard's poetry, The Song of Hárbard)

- Hymiskvia (Hymiskvia) (The song of Hymir, The poem of Hymir)

- Lokasenna (Loki's quarrel, Loki's kink of insults, Loki's dispute)

- Rymskvia (The song of Thrym, The poem of Thrym)

- Völundarkvia (The Völund Song)

- Alvssmál (Alvs' ballad, Alvs' song, Alvs' sayings)

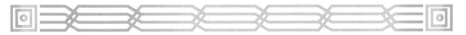

The poems in the Poetic Edda, an Old Norse anthology, react to one of humanity's biggest desires: the quest for roots. These stories of gods, heroes, and monsters, of love, battle, foolishness, and deception, are subtle, nuanced, and evocative but disarmingly straightforward in language. They occupy a universe more primordial in spirit than any other corpus of European mythology. We don't know who wrote them or when they were written. Still, they've captivated philosophers and artists across the board since their rediscovery in the 17th and 18th centuries, who saw these poems as the tantalizing key to a common Northern identity.

Except for a few lines, the Poetic Edda was preserved in a single manuscript known as the Codex Regius, transcribed by an unknown Icelandic scribe in the 1270s and delivered to the Danish court almost four decades later by Lutheran Bishop of Skálholt, Brynjolf Sveinsson. Bishop Brynjolf was certain that this modest book held the hitherto undiscovered source material for Snorri Sturluson's renowned treatise on Norse poetry, known as an edda or poetics, by the Icelandic historian Snorri Sturluson (1179–1241). To differentiate it from Snorri's 'younger' prose work, the Codex Regius was named the Poetic Edda or Elder Edda.

An audience anxious to build a sense of its mythical past greeted translations into Latin, French, and English with enthusiasm. Early adaptations of the Edda poems, such as Thomas Gray's The Descent of Odin, ushered in a craze for Norse mythology in the nineteenth century, which peaked in works like William Morris and Richard Wagner's Ring cycle the mythical substrata, which are based on Eddic stories. The collection's popularity lasted far into the twentieth century, with Ezra Pound, W. H. Auden, and Jorge Luis Borges claiming to be fans. Most notably, J. R. R. Tolkien drew inspiration to create Middle Earth from the Edda.

3.3 Discovery of the Edda

Skalds, or bards or poets, have been associated with Scandinavian courts since the Viking Age, and by the 11th century, these skalds were lar

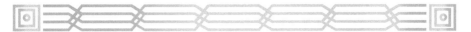

gely Icelandic, Norwegian nobility fleeing persecution-built Iceland in 870 AD. Scandinavians were interested in their history centuries later, and Danish King Frederic III pushed Bishop Brynjólfur Sveinsson to collect all the ancient manuscripts he could locate. In 1643, he found the Prose or Younger Edda, composed in the 12th century by Icelandic nobleman Snorri Sturluson.

The bishop noticed that Sturluson was referencing numerous old skaldic poetry that no longer existed when reading the Prose Edda. Imagine the Bishop's delight when he discovered a literary document including many of the poems Sturluson mentioned. The bishop gave this manuscript of 29 Norse poems Edda Saemundi Multiscii. Like the Prose Edda, the Poetic Edda is Icelandic, although the manuscript dates from about 1270. We don't know who wrote it, but it can't be more than 700 years old.

3.4 Differences Between the Poetic & Prose Eddas

Sturluson's Edda is an intriguing book since it is written in the style of a technical handbook. He demonstrates how to compose Eddic poetry in it. He recounts Old Norse traditions in prose and then provides samples of earlier skalds' poetry descriptions of these legends.

The Poetic Edda is a collection of heroic and legendary poetry. Prose summaries are used to introduce several of the poems. This writing is distinguished from skaldic poetry written by recognized authors about current events and included more complex language and meter. On the other hand, the Poetic Edda is written in a straightforward language and is nameless and objective.

3.5 Þrymskviða

One of the numerous individual poems of Eddic literature surviving in the Codex Regius is rymskvia (Old Norse: "Lay of rym"), sometimes wri-

tten Thrymskvitha. Scholars believe it is one of the most recent Eddic poems because of its ballad form, end-stopped style, and exceptional preservation.

It tells the story of how the giant Rym kidnaps Mjölnir, Thor's hammer, and demands marriage to the goddess Freyja in exchange for returning the weapon. Of course, Freyja doesn't want anything to do with Rym, so Thor disguises himself and approaches Rym as Freyja. The story's hilarity stems mostly from the bride's bizarre behavior during the bridal feast, during which "she" consumes an entire cow, eight fish, and three jugs of mead.

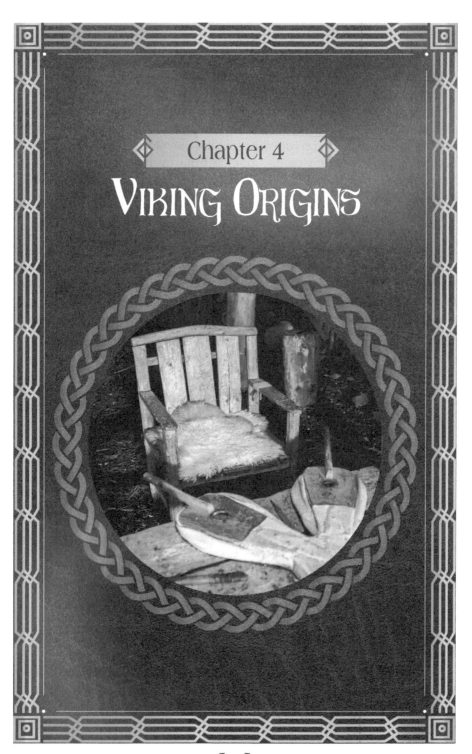

Chapter 4

VIKING ORIGINS

Chapter 4: Viking Origins

The Vikings, also known as Norsemen or Northmen, were Scandinavian maritime warriors who invaded and occupied large portions of Europe during the 9th and 11th centuries, having a tremendous impact on European history. A mix of circumstances, ranging from overpopulation at home to the relative helplessness of victims abroad, likely drove these pagan Danish, Norwegian, and Swedish warriors to carry out their attacks.

Landowning chieftains and clan chiefs, their servants, freemen, and any enthusiastic young clan members seeking adventure and loot abroad made comprised the Vikings. These Scandinavians were independent farmers on the land but robbers and pillagers at sea. The Scandinavian kingdoms seem to have had an almost limitless supply of workforce during the Viking era, and capable commanders who could organize groups of soldiers into conquering bands and armies were common in these people.

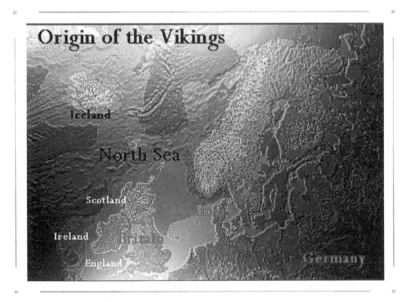

Although the specific ethnic makeup of Viking forces is uncertain in some situations, the Swedes may be blamed for the Vikings' advance in the

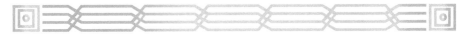

Baltic regions and Russia. The Norwegians were responsible for the nonmilitary colonization of the Orkney Islands, the Faroe Islands, and Iceland.

4.1 Who Were the Vikings?

They were not a "race" bound by bonds of shared ancestry or patriotism, and they could not be identified by any special sense of "Viking-ness," contrary to popular belief. Although there are allusions in historical documents of Finnish, Estonian, and Saami Vikings, the majority of the Vikings whose actions are well known originate from the territories now known as Denmark, Norway, and Sweden. Their common ground–and what distinguished them from the Europeans they encountered–was that they were from another country that was not "civilized" in the local sense and, most crucially, that they were not Christians.

The exact reasons for the Vikings' departure from their homeland are unclear; some have argued that it was due to congestion, although the earliest Vikings were looking for money instead of land. In the eighth century A.D., Europe was growing richer, which fostered the growth of commercial centers such as Dorestad and Quentovic on the Continent as Hamwic (now Southampton), London, Ipswich, and York in England. Scandinavian furs were greatly sought after in the new trading markets. Still, Scandinavians learned about new sailing technology and the rising wealth and internal conflicts among several kingdoms via their trade with Europeans. Viking forefathers–pirates that preyed on merchant ships in the Baltic Sea–would utilize this knowledge to expand their fortune-seeking activities into the North Sea and even beyond.

4.2 Early Viking Raids

In 793, an attack on the Lindisfarne monastery off Northumberland, England, kicked off the Viking Age. Even though the assailants–most likely Norwegians that sailed straight from across the North Sea–did not destroy the monastery, the attack shook the European ecclesiastical system to its core.

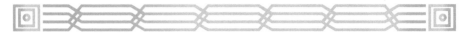

The Vikings limited themselves to hit-and-run attacks on coastal sites in the British Isles (especially Ireland) and Europe for many decades (the trading center of Dorestad, 80 kilometers from the North Sea, became a frequent target after 830). After the death of Louis the Pious, emperor of Frankia (modern-day France and Germany) in 840, his son Lothar enlisted the help of a Viking fleet in a power struggle with his brothers. Other Vikings soon discovered that Frankish rulers were ready to pay them large amounts of money to keep them from harming their civilians, making Frankia an appealing target for further Viking action.

4.3 Conquests in the British Isles

Ireland, Scotland, and England had become key targets for Viking colonization and attacks by the mid-ninth century. The Northern Isles of Scotland (Shetland and the Orkneys), the Hebrides, and most mainland Scotland were conquered by Vikings. They established Ireland's earliest trade towns, including Dublin, Waterford, Wexford, Wicklow, and Limerick. They utilized their coastal base to launch raids inside Ireland and over the Irish Sea to England.

East Anglia and Northumberland were overrun by Viking forces (mainly Danish), and Mercia was demolished. At the same time, King Alfred the Great, of Wessex, became the only ruler in England to beat a Danish army in 871 decisively. After leaving Wessex, the Danes settled in what is now known as "Danelaw," a region to the north. Many of them became farmers and merchants, establishing York as a major trading center. English troops headed by descendants of Alfred of Wessex started reconquering Scandinavian portions of England in the first half of the 10th century; the last Scandinavian monarch, Erik Bloodaxe, was banished and slain about 952, firmly unifying the English into one kingdom.

4.4 Viking Settlements: Europe and Beyond

Throughout the ninth century, Viking forces were active on the European continent, assaulting Nantes (on the French coast) in 842 and attacking cities as far inland as Paris, Limoges, Orleans, Tours, and Nimes. In 844, Vikings assaulted Seville (then under Arab authority), and in 859, they looted Pisa, despite being pummeled by an Arab navy on their way back north. In 911, the West Frankish monarch handed Rouen and its environs to a Viking leader named Rollo in return for the latter's refusal to allow other attackers to cross the Seine. Normandy, or "country of the Northmen," is the name given to this area of northern France.

Scandinavians (mostly Norwegians) started colonizing Iceland in the ninth century, an island in the North Atlantic where no one had yet settled in considerable numbers. Some Vikings (including the fabled Erik the Red) traveled even farther west, to Greenland, by the late 10th century. According to subsequent Icelandic history, some of the early Viking immigrants in Greenland (perhaps led by the Viking hero Leif Eriksson, son of Erik the Red) may have been the first Europeans to find and explore North America. They erected a temporary hamlet at L'Anse aux Meadows in modern-day Newfoundland, which they named Vinland (Wine-land). There is scant proof of Viking activity in the New World beyond that, and they did not establish permanent colonies.

4.5 Danish Dominance

In the mid-tenth century, Harald Bluetooth's tenure as king of a newly unified, strong, and Christianized Denmark signaled the beginning of a second Viking period. Large-scale raids commanded by royal commanders wrought devastation on Europe's coastlines, especially in England, where the line of kings descended from Alfred the Great was unraveling. Harald's rebellious son, Sven Forkbeard, conducted assaults on England in 991 and eventually captured the whole country in 1013, putting King Ethelred into exile. The next year, Sven died, leaving his son Knut (or Canute) in command of a North Sea Scandinavian kingdom that comprised England, Denmark, and Norway.

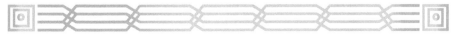

After Knut's death, his two sons succeeded him, but by 1042, both had died, and Edward the Confessor, the son of the previous (non-Danish) monarch, returned from exile and recaptured the English crown from the Danes. After Edward's death (without heirs) in 1066, Harold Godwinson, Edward's strongest powerful noble, claimed the crown. Near York, Harold's army stopped an invasion led by Harald Hardrada, Norway's last major Viking king. Still, it was destroyed two weeks later by William, Duke of Normandy (himself a descendent of Scandinavian immigrants in northern France). Despite repeated Danish threats, William, who was anointed King of England on Christmas Day in 1066, could preserve the kingdom.

4.6 End of the Viking Age

The events of 1066 in England brought the Viking Age to a close. By that time, all Scandinavian countries had converted to Christianity, and what little remained of Viking "culture" had been assimilated into Christian Europe's culture. Viking traces may also be traced today in the Scandinavian roots of certain lexicons and place names in spaces they inhabited, such as northern England, Scotland, and Russia. The Vikings left a significant corpus of literature in Iceland, known as the Icelandic sagas, in which they commemorated their biggest conquests.

Even though the people of Scandinavia had a similar heritage and shared parts of culture such as art and house—and boatbuilding, the vast geographical variations across many of the locations meant that groups lived in quite different ways and faced very distinct issues.

While the Gulf Stream warmed the Norwegian coast, a spine of mountains running north-south divided Norway and Sweden, with few crossings. The northern kingdoms were geographically distinct entities that could not be claimed to be entirely ruled by their purported monarchs even at the end of the Viking Age.

Between 600 and 800, phonological changes in Scandinavian languages occurred, distinguishing them from southern Germanic neighbors Lapps

or Slavs and consolidating the Norse identity and shared culture of Sweden, Norway, and Denmark.Separate Jarls administered provinces, and the earliest pirates claimed to be from Hordaland (those who assassinated the king's reeve at Dorchester in 789) or Vestfold (those who raided Aquitaine in 840), rather than Norway.

The family was the traditional unit of society. It was a much broader concept than it is today, encompassing multiple generations and all of their descendants who would work on the family farm or business for the good of all. In longhouses, they would often live and work together.

There is little evidence that population pressure or a lack of land forced Scandinavian men to flee their homeland. Still, it's possible that powerful and threatening neighbors made it an appealing proposition. It's also possible that the Norse society's three-tier caste structure made it difficult for poor Jarls or freemen to find marriages. This was another driving factor, with young men going abroad searching for enslaved women to function as concubines.

Scandinavian civilization was pagan in terms of religion, worshipping a pantheon of gods and engaging in sacrificial rites, including human sacrifice. Their major deities were the gods of war, Odin and Thor, and a warrior had to die in battle to ascend to Valhalla and join Odin. With no shortage of inter-regional fighting, Norsemen never lacked skill or ferocity in combat, and sea-borne raiding may be considered a logical development when paired with great ship-building abilities.

4.7 England

Desultory raiding occurred in England in the late eighth century (notably the raid on the monastery of Lindisfarne [Holy Island] in 793), but raiding became more serious in 865 when a force led by Ragnar Lothbrok's sons — Halfdan, Inwaer (Ivar the Boneless), and possibly Hubba (Ubbe) — conquered the ancient kingdoms of East Anglia and Northumbria and reduced Mercia to ashes. It was, however, unable to defeat Alfred the Great, of Wessex,

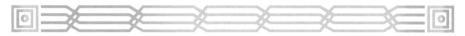

with whom a ceasefire was struck in 878, which became the foundation of a treaty in or shortly after 886. This acknowledged that Denmark controlled a large portion of England. Alfred was eventually successful despite being pressured by new Viking armies from 892 to 899. The spirit of Wessex remained unbroken enough for his son Edward, the Elder, to begin the reconquest of Danish England. Small Danish states on former Mercian and East Anglian land had fallen before his death in 924. The more distant Northumbria resisted much longer, partly under the leadership of Vikings from Ireland, but Eadred eventually extinguished the Scandinavian dominance there in 954. In 980, Viking invasions on England resumed, and the nation eventually became part of Canute's dominion. Nonetheless, the native house was quietly restored in 1042, and the Viking menace was stopped by Canute II's unsuccessful passes during William I's reign. The Scandinavian conquests in England left indelible effects on the social structure, accent, place names, and the names of its inhabitants.

4.8 The Western Seas, Vinland, and Ireland

Scandinavian advances in the western oceans reached almost every possible point. From about the year 900, settlers flocked into Iceland, establishing colonies in Greenland and attempting to colonize North America. Settlements appeared on the Orkney, Faroe, Shetland Islands, the Hebrides, and the Isle of Man around the same period.

The early Viking trips to North America, which they dubbed Vinland, are described in two Norse sagas: Grnlendinga saga ("Saga of the Greenlanders") and Eirks saga raua ("Erik the Red's Saga") (land of wild grapes). Bjarni Herjólfsson, whose Greenland-bound ship was blown westward off course in 985 and likely circled the coastline of eastern Canada before returning to Greenland, was the first European to witness mainland North America, according to the Grnlendinga saga. According to legend, over 1000 men commanded by Leif Eriksson, son of Erik the Red, set out to pursue the country glimpsed by Bjarni and ended themselves in eastern Canada. Leif's brothers are claimed to have led other journeys, while another headed by Icelandic merchant Thorfinn Karlsefni has stayed in Vinland for three years.

Leif is Vinland's unintentional discoverer in Eirks saga raua. All future exploration is assigned to Thorfinn and his wife, Gudrid. Archaeological discoveries near L'Anse aux Meadows (Newfoundland and Labrador) proved that the Vikings traveled at least as far south as areas where grapes grew wild, pointing to the fact that the Vikings first confronted North America in eastern New Brunswick.

Invasion of Ireland by Scandinavians dates back to 795, when Rechru, an unidentified island, was destroyed. Fighting continued after that, and Scandinavian kingdoms were established in Dublin, Limerick, and Waterford, even though the indigenous frequently held their own. For a period, the kings of Dublin felt powerful enough to move abroad, and many of them reigned in both Dublin and Northumberland in the early 10th century. With the terrible loss of the Irish Scandinavians, assisted by the Earl of Orkney and some native Irish at the Battle of Clontarf in 1014, the possibility of Ireland being united under Scandinavian leadership faded. The Scandinavians were still prominent (albeit Christianized) in Dublin, Waterford, Limerick, Wexford, and Cork when the English invaded Ireland in the 12th century.

4.9 The Carolingian Empire and France

Outside of Normandy, Viking colonization was never as widespread in the well-defended Carolingian realm as in the British Isles. Scandinavian impact on continental languages and institutions was minimal. Sporadic raiding continued until the end of the Viking era, and colonies on the Seine River formed the germ of the duchy of Normandy in the 10th century, the only lasting Viking success in what had been Charlemagne's realm.

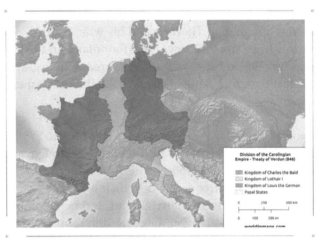

Division of the Carolingian
Empire - Treaty of Verdun (846)

Kingdom of Charles the Bald
Kingdom of Lothair I
Kingdom of Louis the German
Papal States

0   250   500 km
0   100   200 mi
worldinmans com

Further south, in the Iberian Peninsula and throughout the Mediterranean beaches, the Vikings attacked regularly but left little lasting damage.

4.10 Eastern Europe

The eastern Viking invasion was probably less violent than the Atlantic Viking expansion. Although there was no doubt periodic raiding in the Baltic, and the idiom "to go on the East-Viking" meant to engage in such action, no Viking state was created in that region with the sword.

The largest eastern march of the Scandinavians was the one that took them into Russia's heartland. The degree of this invasion is difficult to determine. Although the Scandinavians were once prominent in Novgorod, Kiev, and other cities, they were quickly absorbed by the Slavonic populace, to whom they gave the name Rus, "Russians."

Two of the Rus' commercial contracts with the Greeks are recorded in the Primary Chronicle under the numbers 912 and 945; the Rus signatories had unmistakably Scandinavian names. However, like their western counter

parts, the Rus launched plundering expeditions occasionally. Their existence as a distinct people did not last much more than 1050.

A fresh Viking push toward the east seems to have begun in the first half of the 11th century. Those who accompanied Yngvarr on his trips are recorded on several Swedish runic stones. These expeditions were to the east, but only legends about their exact destination and purpose have survived. Another activity of the Scandinavians in the east was mercenary service at Constantinople (Istanbul), where they constituted the Byzantine emperor's Varangian Guard.

The Viking leader became a historical character after the 11th century. Denmark became a conquering power, integrating the most turbulent sections of its populace into its royal army. Norway and Sweden had no more force for the exterior expedition, and Denmark became a conquering power. Before becoming King of Norway in 1015, Olaf II Haraldsson was essentially the last Viking leader in the old autonomous tradition.

4.11 Scientists Raid DNA to Discover Vikings' Genetic Roots

Vikings were portrayed in popular culture as strong, flaxen-haired Scandinavian warriors who pillaged northern European shores aboard sleek wooden warships. However, despite ancient sagas that honor nautical heroes with diverse genealogies, the contemporary notion that Vikings were a unique ethnic or geographical group of people with a "pure" genetic bloodline persists. Nonetheless, it is still commemorated by numerous white nationalist organizations that utilize the Vikings' alleged supremacy to justify hatred, propagating the stereotype in the process.

Now, massive ancient DNA research published today in Nature reveals the full genetic variation of the people we name Vikings, confirming and expanding on what historical and archaeological evidence has previously shown about this cosmopolitan and politically strong group of merchants and explorers.

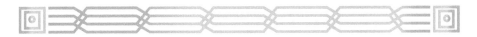

4.12 Far-Flung Connections

According to a DNA study, Vikings have ancestors from hunter-gatherers, farmers, and tribes from the Eurasian steppe. The study also identifies three main genetically varied hot areas where individuals from different places mingled throughout the era: one in Denmark and one each on the Swedish islands of Gotland and land. At the time, all three places were supposed to have been bustling commercial hubs.

However, even though Vikings left—and in some instances returned to—Scandinavia, DNA evidence suggests that they did not interact as much inside the wider Scandinavian area as they did beyond it, mingling with a diverse variety of peoples.
"The DNA data clearly shows that Vikings are not a homogeneous group of people," Willerslev argues. "Many Vikings are mixed persons," having heritage from Southern Europe and Scandinavia, or even a mix of Sami (Indigenous Scandinavian) and European origin.

4.13 Unbound by Ethnicity

The topics also have less in common with current Scandinavians than you may imagine. Only 15 to 30% of modern-day Swedes have ancestors who lived in the same location 1,300 years ago, indicating even greater movement and mixing of peoples following the Viking period. Residents of the area during the Viking Age did not have the classic Scandinavian appearance: The ancient Danes, for example, had darker hair and eyes on average than a randomly picked sample of current Danes.

The DNA evidence backs up what historians and archaeologists have long suspected: Vikings were a heterogeneous people who were not limited by country or ethnicity. "It's fantastic research," says archaeologist Jesse Byock, who directs the Mosfell Archaeological Project in Iceland and professor at the University of California, Los Angeles. He was not a part of the genetic study. "It adds to what we already know about the Vikings while also reinforcing practically everything we already know."

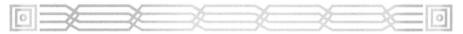

According to Miguel Vilar, a former senior program officer for the National Geographic Society, the results depict a complicated picture of Viking history, which runs opposed to current concepts of nationalism and cultural identity. He claims that "DNA doesn't always fit easily into [preconceived] categories." (The research did not include Vilar, the chief scientist for the NGS Genographic Project.)

4.14 Bands of Brothers

The analysis indicated significant familial relationships, despite the Viking canopy being large. Four brothers were recognized and put side by side in a funeral at Salme, Estonia, where 41 Swedish men were interred after a fight with two boats and their weapons. Researchers also uncovered a second-degree familial tie between a Viking buried in a Danish cemetery and another buried in Oxford, England, demonstrating how mobile Viking families were at the time.

On the other hand, the huge DNA analysis is unable to answer the issue of how the Viking craze arose in the first place. What brought these folks together, if not ethnicity? Due to technical advancements, was it the capacity to construct seaworthy vessels and conduct war effectively on the water, or were there other variables at play?

According to Zori, "people may accept and adapt to prevailing cultural patterns of survival...Being a Viking was one of the key techniques of surviving and being successful economically and politically for whatever reason."

Researchers may now broaden their hunt for Viking ancestors because of recent evidence that individuals were genetically varied at least 442 Viking Era. Byock explains, "This is beautifully enormous research, yet it's just 450 skeletons." "It's a big first step." He thinks this is only the start of a larger examination of the era's genetic history.

"It's probably true that genetics is more credible than Viking sagas," Zori says. However, he claims that only time and further study will complete the picture.

Now comes the difficult task of coping with the large study's consequences and merging literary and archaeological data with the new DNA findings. There's still a lot to discover about how the cultural catalysts known as Vikings lived and moved and what happened to them on their quest for adventure and power. "Migration has always played a role in human history," Zori explains. "There's more stuff out there," says the author.

4.15 A Brief History of the Vikings

Invaders, predators, and barbarians—the Vikings are sometimes depicted as one-dimensional warriors whose accomplishments are limited to looting and raiding. But where did the Vikings come from, and were they godless, murderous pagans?

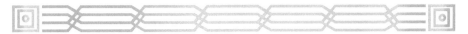

Armed attackers assaulted the defenseless monastery of St. Cuthbert on Lindisfarne in 793, bringing panic to the Northumbrian coast. The scared monks stood powerless and helpless as the attackers made off with a load of gold and a slew of hostages. It was the first known raid by the Vikings, seaborne pirates from Scandinavia who preyed on coastal settlements in north-western Europe for more than two centuries, earning a reputation as ruthless warriors.

Those who wrote about the Viking invasions—in other words, their victims—emphasized this picture. Following the Lindisfarne raid, the Anglo-Saxon cleric Alcuin of York described the church as "spattered with the blood of the priests of God, despoiled of all its ornaments... given as a prey to pagan peoples," and subsequent (mainly Christian) writers and chroniclers missed few opportunities to demonize the (mainly pagan) Vikings.

Even though the Vikings were known for their destructive and violent assaults, ranging from small-scale raids on churches to large-scale battles involving thousands of troops, they were part of a rich and sometimes intelligent Scandinavian society. They were raiders, but they were also traders, reaching as far east as Russia's rivers and the Caspian Sea; explorers, sending ships far across the Atlantic to land on the North American coast five centuries before Columbus; poets, writing powerful verse and prose sagas, and artists, creating works of breathtaking beauty.

The Vikings' reputation as raiders and plunderers had long been established. It's long past to restore their reputation as merchants, storytellers, explorers, missionaries, artists, and kings.

When and Where Did the Vikings Come from?

The Vikings came from today's areas, Denmark, Norway, and Sweden (although centuries before they became unified countries). Their country was mostly rural, with few settlements. The overwhelming majority made a meager living from agriculture or fishing near the shore. In the 7th and 8th centuries, advances in maritime technology allowed vessels to be driven by sails rather than oars alone. Longships, fast shallow-drafted boats that could travel coastal and inland waterways and land on beaches, were created by adding them to vessels composed of overlapping boards ('clinker-built').

It's unknown what prompted bands of men to sail across the North Sea in longships to follow their local chieftain. It might have been localized overcrowding because plots were split to the idea that households could hardly make ends meet; political instability, as chieftains struggled for power; or tales carried home by merchants of the riches to be found in trade communities farther west. It was most likely a mix of all three. However, the first raiding group attacked Lindisfarne in 793, and within a few years, other Viking bands invaded Scotland (794), Ireland (795), and France (796).

They were not referred to as Vikings by their victims. That name emerged later, becoming popular in the 11th century and likely stemming from the term Vik, which means 'bay' or 'inlet' in the Old Norse language used by the Vikings. Instead, they were termed) Pagani ('pagans'), Dani ('Danes'), or simply Normanni ('Northmen') — there was no sense at that time.

A portion of the Great Army commanded by Guthrum crossed the boundary in early January 878 and surprised Alfred at the royal estate of Chippenham. Alfred escaped and spent months hiding in the Somerset marshes of Athelney. It seemed like Wessex's — and England's — independence could be coming to an end. Despite the difficulties, Alfred assembled a new army, fought the Vikings at Edington, and compelled Guthrum to accept Christian baptism. He was the first native English monarch to be given the appellation 'the Great' for his success in preserving his realm.

For 80 years, England was split between the Wessex monarchs in the south and south-west and land controlled by the Vikings in the Midlands and north. The last of the Viking monarchs, Erik Bloodaxe, was exiled and slain in 954, and the kings of Wessex became the rulers of a unified England. Even yet, Viking (and particularly Danish) habits endured for a long time, and traces of Scandinavian DNA may still be discovered in an area known as the Danelaw for centuries.

By the mid-eleventh century, Denmark, Norway, and Sweden had become unified kingdoms, and the attacks had ceased. In the early 11th century, a last spurt of activity occurred when royal-sponsored expeditions succeeded in reconquering England and installing Danish rulers on the throne (including, most notably, Canute, who ruled an empire in England, Denmark, and

Norway, but who almost certainly did not command the tide to go out, as a folk tale alleges). Large swaths of Scotland (particularly Orkney), Ireland, and Normandy, France, remained under Viking dominion (wherein 911 King Charles the Simple had granted land to a Norwegian chieftain, Rollo, the ancestor of William the Conqueror). They also ruled over a substantial portion of modern-day Ukraine and Russia, as Swedish Vikings invaded in the ninth century and built republics centered on Novgorod and Kyiv.

Where Did Vikings Settle and Live?

However, this was hardly the whole of the Viking world. The same nautical aggressiveness that drove them to raid (and eventually conquer) inhabited territories also drove them to seek out new coastlines to settle on. Vikings most likely discovered the Faroe Islands in the ninth century, and they utilized them as a stepping stone to travel farther west over the Atlantic.

A series of Viking expeditions passed through Iceland in the mid-ninth century, and in the year 872, immigrants headed by Ingólf Arnarson arrived on the island. They created a fiercely autonomous society and had no official loyalty to the Norwegian rulers. The Althing, an assembly of Iceland's top men who gathered each summer in a plain near a large fissure in a ring of hills in the island's center, was the republic's ultimate governing body from 930. It has a good claim to being the oldest parliament in the world.

Other important evidence of the Viking civilizations' creativity may also be found in Iceland. The slendingabók, a 12th-century history of Iceland, and the Landnámabók, an account of the island's early colonization, are among the oldest works of history written by Vikings themselves (with the names of each of the first settlers and the land they took).

The collection of sagas known as the slendingasögur or Icelandic Family Sagas is more significant—and startling for people who think of the Vikings as one-dimensional warriors. Alliances, feuds, betrayals, and murders occur against a background of recognizable elements that may still be found today.

Who Was the Most Famous Viking?

Ivar the Boneless, a legendary warrior and one of the 'Great Heathen Army' commanders that arrived in East Anglia in 865 and conquered the kingdoms of Northumbria and East Anglia, is recognized as the founder of the Viking kingdom of Dublin's royal dynasty.

It's unclear how Ivar earned the moniker 'the Boneless'; however, some have speculated that it was due to his extraordinary warfare flexibility or because he suffered from a degenerative muscle disease that forced him to be carried around. We'll never know until his corpse is ever retrieved — which would be tough if he was indeed 'boneless.'

Vikings and Religion: What Gods Did They Believe in?

Another drama set in Iceland focused on the shift of Viking society away from martial chieftainships. Scandinavian Viking communities received Christianity later than many other regions of Europe. The kings of France had accepted Christianity by the early sixth century and the Anglo-Saxon kings of England largely in the seventh. Christian missionaries only arrived in southern Scandinavia in the ninth century and made little progress there till Harald Bluetooth of Denmark accepted baptism in around 960. Harald had become a Christian following a classic piece of Viking theatre: a drunken debate about who was more powerful, Odin and Thor or the new Christian God and his son, Jesus, over the feasting table.

Iceland remained steadfastly pagan, devoted to ancient gods such as Odin, the All-Father, a one-eyed deity who had given his other eye in return for knowledge of runes, and Thor, the thunder god with his mighty hammer Mjolnir, who was particularly popular among warriors.

To avert civil strife, Iceland converted to Christianity. Competing pagan and Christian groups threatened to destabilize the Althing and split Iceland into hostile republics. Rival groups appealed to Iceland's most powerful official, the law-speaker Thorgeir Thorkelsson, during the Althing's assembly in the year 1000. As a pagan, he was expected to choose the old gods, but after a whole day of deliberation, he decided that all Icelanders would be Christian from now on. A few exceptions were allowed, such as the consumption of horsemeat, a popular delicacy that was also linked with pagan rites.

What Was Valhalla, and How Did Vikings Get There?

What two items would a Viking most want in Valhalla, the hall of dead warriors, in the afterlife? Of course, there will be feasting and fighting.

According to BBC History Revealed magazine, if a Norse warrior was selected to die by the fabled Valkyries, he wished to be welcomed into Valhalla by the god Odin, a beautiful hall with a ceiling covered with golden shields, spears for rafters, and so big that 540 doorways lined its walls. The honored dead, called the Einherjar, practiced their war skills against one another all day in preparation for Ragnarök—the end of the world—then their wounds mysteriously healed, and they celebrated as only as the end of the world Vikings could.

Their drinking horns were never empty because of Heidrun, a goat on Valhalla's roof who ate from a particular tree and made the best mead. And there was always enough meat thanks to Shrmnir, a boar that came back to life after each slaughter and could be cooked again and over.

A Viking had to die in combat to join the Einherjar, and even then, they only had a 50:50 chance. The half who was not selected to travel to Valhalla instead went to Freya's meadow to give their companionship to the ladies who died as maidens.

The elderly and ill were sent to Hel, the underworld. Though there was a specific area of suffering prepared for murderers, adulterers, and oath-breakers, where a monstrous dragon devoured on their bodies, it wasn't quite as horrible as the name indicates.

Where Did the Vikings Travel to?

Likewise, Iceland served as the starting point for the Vikings' most far-flung expeditions. Erik the Red, a fiery chieftain who had previously been banished from Norway for his father's role in a homicide, was deported from Iceland in 982 for his role in another murder. He'd heard rumors of land to the west and set off with a small party of buddies to find it. What he discovered was much beyond his wildest dreams. Greenland, which lies just 300 kilometers west of Iceland, is the world's biggest island, with fjords [deep, narrow, and vast sea or lake drains with high hills on three sides] and rich meadows that must have reminded Erik of his Scandinavian roots. He returned to Iceland, assembled 25 shiploads of immigrants, and founded a new Viking colony in Greenland, which lasted until the 15th century.

Leif, Erik's son, outdid his father. After hearing from another Viking Greenlander, Bjarni Herjolfsson, Leif, traveled to check for himself that he had discovered land much farther west. He and his crew were traveling somewhere near the coast of North America around the year 1002. They discovered a glacier, hilly coast, then a forested one, and ultimately Vinland, an area of lush meadows. Despite their intention to establish a new colony there, unlike Iceland or Greenland, it was already occupied, and native Americans' animosity and their tiny numbers (Greenland at the time probably had approximately

3,000 Vikings) meant it was abandoned quickly. They were, however, the first Europeans to arrive in (and dwell in) the Americas, arriving over five centuries before Christopher Columbus.

Erik's achievements were only preserved for generations in two sagas, The Saga of the Greenlanders and Erik the Red's Saga. Despite efforts to deduce its location from information included in the sagas, the location of Vinland remained mysterious. It was even debatable if the Vikings had made it to North America. Then, in the early 1960s, Helge Ingstad, a Norwegian adventurer, and his archaeologist wife, Anne Stine, discovered the ruins of old dwellings in L'Anse aux Meadows, Newfoundland, Canada. Fragments of wrought iron (many of them nails, most likely from a ship) quickly revealed that this was a Viking colony that the local inhabitants could not make. Even though it was probably too tiny to represent the major Vinland colony, it was nonetheless a remarkable confirmation of what the sagas had indicated. The legend of Leif Erikson as a famous explorer and discoverer of new places was unmistakably established.

Did Viking Shield-Maidens Exist?

According to BBC History Revealed magazine, sorry, Vikings fans: historians can't decide whether Norse warrior women like Lagertha existed. While historical descriptions of shield maidens, or skjaldmaer, exist, virtually all of them may be rejected as untrustworthy, fictitious, symbolic, or more myth than fact.

Nonetheless, tantalizing signs and puzzling discoveries — like relics depicting women wielding swords, spears, and shields — have bolstered the theory that Viking women fought alongside men. Women in Denmark strived "such ardently to be adept in fighting that they may have been assumed to have unsexed themselves," according to Danish historian Saxo Grammaticus in the 12th century. Meanwhile, in 2017, researchers uncovered that a warrior's burial from the 10th century, which was loaded with weaponry, really belonged to a woman.

What Was a Viking Sunstone?

According to BBC History Revealed magazine, the Vikings were excellent sailors who traveled as far as Russia and North America, but their navigational methods have not always been fully understood. A mysterious sunstone referenced in a medieval Icelandic tale was dismissed as a myth until an opaque crystal made of Iceland spar was found amid the navigation equipment of a drowned Tudor shipwreck.

Surprisingly, scientists have shown that when Iceland spar is held up to the sky, it produces a solar compass that tells the Sun's position via concentric bands of polarized light, even under dense cloud cover or after night. This may have been the mysterious sunstone that guided Vikings like 'Lucky' Leif Erikson to Newfoundland, and its use may have continued until the end of the 16th century.

THE VIKING ARMY AND FAMOUS BATTLES

Chapter 5: The Viking Army and Famous Battles

Some of the most famous fights in British history occurred during the Viking era. There was Edington (AD 878) when Alfred the Great triumphed against the odds over a portion of a massive Danish invasion force; Brunanburh (AD 937), when Alfred's grandson Athelstan stamped his authority on the British Isles; as well as Stamford Bridge (1066), where Harald Hardrada's Viking army's bones were left to whiten on the field, picked clean by carrion birds.

On the other hand, the Viking Age spanned over three centuries, from the end of the ninth century to the middle of the eleventh. Sources mention at least 50 pitched battles in England alone during this period and many raids, sieges, and naval conflicts. Over the ages, most of these have been mostly forgotten.

On the other hand, many of them were instrumental in forming the embryonic kingdoms of England and Scotland. So, here are some Viking-era battles: confrontations that shaped Britain's future while underappreciated and generally forgotten.

5.1 The Battle of Edington

Britain was no stranger to abrupt, destructive Viking assaults in the 9th century. However, things took on a new, dangerous turn in 865, when the Vikings grew even bolder and assembled the Great Heathen Army, a massive invasion army. They didn't come to plunder an isolated village; they came to conquer it. The Vikings swept over Anglo-Saxon England over several years, toppling different kingdoms until they met Alfred the Great, King of Wessex.

Alfred seemed to be another victim of the Viking invaders at first. His army was annihilated, and the king was relegated to the position of an outlaw, fighting the Vikings in guerilla warfare. During this time, legend has it that a disguised Alfred sought refuge in the home of a peasant woman, who requested him to care about a batch of bread she was preparing and then reprimanded the unhappy monarch when they burned.

Alfred eventually assembled an army of locals and engaged the Vikings in a terrible battle. The Battle of Edington is the name given to this critical clash. The Anglo-Saxons triumphed resoundingly, and according to a contemporary source, Alfred "overthrew the pagans with tremendous bloodshed." Guthrum, the head of the Viking army, turned to Christianity shortly after, ensuring Alfred's status as a great English ruler.

5.2 The Battle of Maldon

In 991, under King Aethelred the Unready, another bloody battle erupted, but this time the Anglo-Saxons did not fare as well. The attacks resumed in the late 10th century, after a lengthy period when the Vikings seemed to have been less of a menace to England. Some thought paying them off was the best way to deal with them, while others were outraged, feeling that Viking brutality should be answered with violence.

Byrhtnoth, a royal official in Essex, was one of these fighters, rallying his soldiers against Viking warriors as they sailed up the Blackwater River.

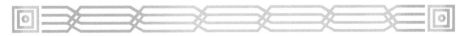

Due to geography, the Vikings were compelled to cluster on a tiny slice of land in the river, which was most likely Northey Island. However, Byrhtnoth's bravery prevented him from taking advantage of his situation. In the sake of fair combat, he consented to the Vikings' plea to be permitted to pass from the island to the mainland without being picked off.

The battle began. The overly-chivalrous Byrhtnoth was killed and his army was defeated. Following this, the English agreed to pay the Viking "tax," or Danegeld, to avert future bloodshed. At the same time, Byrhtnoth's disastrous fight inspired the Battle of Maldon, a magnificent work of Old English poetry.

England was regularly assaulted by Viking invaders from the 9th century forward.

5.3 The Battle of Assandun

The Battle of Hastings is the most well-known 11th-century conflict. However, a few decades before 1066, in the year 1016, a foreign army charged into the nation, overthrowing the previous nobility and establishing a new royal family. The Battle of Assandun resulted in a dynasty of Viking rulers that lasted just a few generations. Assandun and its aftermath are only known today because the kingdom was dominated by William the Conqueror 50 years later.

Edmund Ironside, son of Aethelred the Unready, who had been forced into exile in Europe by a previous invading group of Vikings, was the commander of the English warriors at the time. When Aethelred came to reclaim his realm, it sparked an epic power struggle between the Anglo-Saxon monarchs and the Viking pretender, Cnut the Great, who would become legendary.

Cnut and his invading army faced forces headed by Aethelred's son, Edmund Ironside, who ascended to the throne after Aethelred's death in April 1016. The scene was prepared for a showdown between Edmund, the new king, and Cnut, who desired his newly placed crown. Cnut's victory against

Edmund at the Battle of Assandun in October 1016 brought things ahead. Cnut became the ultimate Viking King of England after Edmund's death just a few weeks later.

5.4 The Battle of York

When the Vikings' Great Heathen Army arrived in England in 865 A.D., the Battle of York was fought. Ivar, the Viking chieftain, led this army to East Anglia for the first time.

East Anglians petitioned for peace and promised to provide the soldiers with food. Ivar and his army marched north to the realm of Northumbria the next winter.

The Northumbrians were caught off guard when they were attacked in the winter. They were beaten in the Battle of York that followed, and the Vikings essentially took over York.

The Vikings won the fight, and the Northumbrian kingdom ended as a result.

5.5 The Battle of Englefield

On December 31, 870 AD, this fight took place. It was fought between the West Saxons and the Vikings. It happened in the Berkshire town of Englefield. The Vikings had taken over the kingdom of Wessex before the conflict.

They camped in Reading before riding to Englefield. The Vikings were headed by Sidrac, while Aethelwulf of Berkshire led the West Saxons. The West Saxons triumphed, but the Vikings suffered huge casualties.

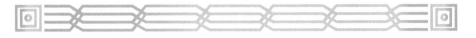

5.6 The Battle of Ashdown

On the 8th of January 871 AD, this fight took place in Berkshire, to the northwest of Reading. The English people of Wessex were pitted against Viking invaders from Scandinavia in this conflict.

The Danes sailed up the Thames River to Reading, Berkshire, in 870. While the English troops were enjoying Christmas, they captured Reading.

Around the 28th of December, the Danes came. The English force was pushed out from Reading, six miles away, to Englefield. Following the English army, the Vikings were routed at Englefield. They returned to Reading.

The Viking army assaulted once again, meeting the Anglo-Saxon force 11 miles outside of Reading. The Vikings were beaten again by the Anglo Saxons led by Alfred the Great, who was just 22 years old.

5.7 The Battle of Brunanburh

In 937, the Battle of Brunanburh took place. It happened between the Anglo-Saxon Kingdom of England and Dublin, Scotland, and Strathclyde on one side and the kingdoms of Ireland, Scotland, and Strathclyde on the other.

Aethelstan, considered as one of the greatest Anglo-Saxon monarchs, commanded the English soldiers. Olaf Guthfrithson, a Viking commander, was the ruler of the Kingdom of Dublin.
Although the Vikings were generally united against the English, Aethelstan was able to enlist the help of some Viking mercenaries.

The Battle of Brunanburh is considered one of the most important Anglo-Saxon engagements. It ended in a clear win for the English, despite terrible losses on both sides.

5.8 The Battle of Clontarf

On April 23, 1014, this fight took place. This battle occurred on the River Tolka, near Clontarf, Ireland. The battle pitted Brian Boru, Ireland's High King, against a Norse-Irish coalition.

The soldiers of Brian Boru were victorious. Thousands of fighters were slaughtered on both sides. In this fight, King Brian Boru was also slain.

5.9 Battle of Stamford Bridge

The fight took place at the hamlet of Stamford Bridge in the East Riding of Yorkshire. It was fought between King Harold II of England's armies and King Harald Hadrada of Norway's Viking army.

On September 25, 1066, the war began. The Viking chieftain, as well as the majority of the Norwegians, were slain in this combat.

This conflict marked the end of the Viking Age.

The English troops won the fight, and the Vikings were slaughtered in large numbers.

The remaining Norwegians, including Harald Hadrada's son, were permitted to return.

5.10 The Battle of Hengest's Hill

Wessex's King Egbert was not a man to be trifled with. He established himself and his empire as Britain's preeminent force in AD 825, destroying the Mercians at Ellendun, near outside Swindon. It was a bloody affair. "Ellen-

dun's stream flowed scarlet with blood, was clogged up with corpses, full with odor," according to a poem fragment.

This was merely one front in Egbert's quest to conquer the rest of Britain's kingdoms. He ravaged Cornwall "from east to west" in AD 815, reminding the still-independent Cornish kingdom of their autonomy's boundaries. On the other hand, the Cornish determined in AD 838 that the moment had come to strike back against West Saxon dominance. They had allies this time — Viking friends.

According to the Anglo-Saxon Chronicle, a "great ship-horde arrived in Cornwall" in AD 838, combining forces with the local Cornish and immediately challenging King Egbert's rule. Egbert led his army into Cornwall, where he used his might at a spot known as Hengest's Hill. This was most likely Kit Hill, the enormous bluff that dominates the Tamar Valley, one of whose flanks is still known as Hingston.

5.11 The Battle of Cynwit

Things were looking bleak for Egbert's grandson, King Alfred, in AD 878. A Viking force commanded by the warlord Guthrum had invaded Wessex, seizing Chippenham and forcing Alfred into exile inside his realm.

The monarch was on the run for many months, hiding in marshes and wild locations. He eventually established a base on the Isle of Athelney in Somerset, from where he led guerilla operations against the Viking occupants. When a second Viking army, headed by the warrior Ubbe, landed in the southwest of England, it must have seemed that the West Saxon dynasty's days were numbered in the double digits.

Odda, the ealdorman of Devon, fought back against Ubbe's troops. The fight that ensued was fought at an undetermined hillfort called 'Cynwit' in the southwest of England, and it was one of the major military reversals of the early Middle Ages. Bishop Asser of Sherborne, King Alfred's historian, described how the West Saxons were besieged within the citadel by the Viking force, without food or water, after retreating behind the clay defenses. However, according to Asser, rather than being weakened by a siege, the West Saxons opted to pursue triumph or a glorious death. They pushed themselves down the hills at daylight, crushing their former besiegers with savagery and forcing the surviving to their ships. Around 1,200 Viking warriors were killed, including Ubbe.

5.12 The Battle of the Holme

Anglo-Saxon and Viking warfare continued after Alfred's death in AD 899. Indeed, no sooner had Alfred's son, Edward, Aethelwold, assumed the throne than he was confronted with a military crisis. Alfred's nephew, revolted against his cousin Edward, believing he had been unjustly overlooked, before escaping to areas of England under Viking authority (swaths of the north and east of the nation known as 'the Danelaw'). He was reportedly greeted with wide arms and crowned "king of the pagans; ruler of the Danes" there.

In the summer of AD 902, the world launched his campaign, sending an army from Viking East Anglia and raiding southern England further than Cricklade and Braydon in Wessex. This was a provocation because Edward (after known as 'the Elder') lost no time gathering an army to follow his cousin back into East Anglia's cold and unforgiving fens.

Who Was Aethelflaed, the Warrior Queen Who Defeated the Vikings?

The fight ensued on the Holme ('island'), and it was a disaster for practically everyone involved. Edward, presumably aware of the terrain's difficulties, ordered a withdrawal, but the Kentish contingent refused. In a panic, Edward dispatched rider after rider (a total of seven) to tell his soldiers to retreat. They failed to withdraw for reasons we will never know.

The belligerents "clashed shields, swung swords, and shook the spear heavily in each hand," according to the sole account we have of the battle. Fighting in the fens' sucking peat bogs, on the other hand, would have been a waking nightmare. The men of Kent would have slid and fallen, crushed in the grasping fens, drowned in the muck and brackish bog-water, floundering through the reed-beds into calamity if they had broken and run, tossing away shields and weapons in their despair. And tragedy it was for the warriors of Kent: The Kentish ealdorman Sigewulf, his relative Sigehelm, and almost all of the Kentish nobles were slaughtered.

However, King Edward had a silver lining: Aethelwold, the imposter, was dead. Who knows what the future would have contained for Aethelwold if he had won the battle of Holme. Instead, a major threat to Edward's power and legitimacy had been eliminated. Edward would go on the offensive in the next decades, capturing all of Viking-held England south of the Humber.

5.13 The Battle of Stanmore

The fight of Stainmore may not have been combating at all, yet it was remembered as such by those who came after it—the old kingdom of Northumbria's final gasp of freedom.

Since AD 866, when the Viking micel here ('great army) seized the city of York, Northumbria has been under Viking rule. Scandinavian culture infiltrated many facets of life in England's most northerly realm during the next nine decades, altering language, clothing, religion, and identity. However, the Northumbrians remained a proud people with a long and illustrious

history, and if pressed, they would choose a foreign Viking monarch to the West Saxon dynasty's rough hand. And this is exactly what they got when Eric Bloodaxe, the former king of Norway, took over the Northumbrian throne in the mid-tenth century.

When Eadred wasn't looking, the Northumbrians welcomed Eric back in AD 952, but he was sent away a second time in AD 954. He crossed the Pennines westward, passing through the hills of Cumbria on the Stainmore pass, presumably in search of the Irish Sea. He never showed up. According to English accounts, Eric died a filthy death on the road, "treacherously slain by Earl Maccus."

However, Scandinavian accounts claim that Eric faced his opponents at the head of an outnumbered army and died the glorious death of the typical Viking commander there on the steep, wind-scoured pass. Eric arrived in Valhalla, greeted by Valkyries, to feast and battle by Odin's side till the end of the world, according to a poem commissioned by his wife: a fitting epitaph for the last king of independent Northumbria.

5.14 The Battle of Dane's Wood

The year 1016 saw a lot of bloodshed. It saw Edmund 'Ironside' take up the sword held ineffectively by his father, Aethelred the Unready, and stand firmly against the threat offered by the Danish prince. Edmund and Cnut fought 7 times that year, 6 of which are well-known, but the seventh was nearly lost to history.

Svein Forkbeard, Cnut's father, had temporarily ascended to the throne of England in the winter of 1013/14. The English throne had returned to the West Saxon line when Svein died unexpectedly—murdered, it was thought, by the evil spirit of St Edmund, the king of East Anglia slaughtered by the Vikings in AD 869. On the other hand, Cnut was not a guy who made claims to authority lightly.

Cnut and Edmund fought large engagements in 1016 in Penselwood in Somerset, Sherston in Wiltshire, London, Brentford in Middlesex, and Otford in Kent (Kent). In all of these battles (save Sherston, which ended in a stalemate), Edmund defeated the Danish opponent, and it must have seemed like Cnut's campaign was about to fizzle out.

The battle of Assandun is widely seen as the turning point in the conflict, paving the way for Cnut to retake the crown that his father had prematurely left. But Edmund was not yet dead, and the English king would have to fight one more battle before laying down his weapons and agreeing to conditions. "Prince, you won fame with the sword north of mighty Danaskógar, but it seemed a slaughter to your followers," the Viking skald Ottar the Black wrote in praise of Cnut in a single stanza of poetry.

Danaskógar means "forest of the Danes," and no place in England has ever been given that name. However, it is known that Edmund and his

army fled to Gloucestershire, where the Forest of Dean, across the Severn, would have given arboreal safety. It's probable that the Old Norse speakers in Cnut's army, chasing Edmund's beaten men into these western forests, heard the name 'Dean' and misinterpreted it as Old English Dena: 'of the Danes,' rather than denu ('valley'). The Forest of Dean was dubbed the Forest of the Danes after being retranslated into Old Norse. It was a land gained and renamed with the sword.

Chapter 6
Asgardians

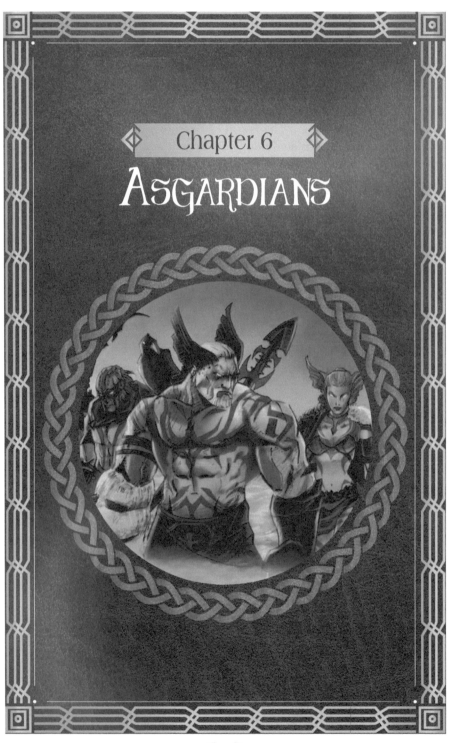

Chapter 6: Asgardians

The Asgardians, sometimes known as the sir, are the residents of Asgard, the home of the gods of Norse mythology. They are an alien species with a humanoid appearance and a highly evolved sort of technology that resembles magic, on which their civilization is based. Odin controlled them and had a reputation as peacekeepers in the Nine Realms for millennia.

The Asgardians are a strong warrior species whose religion is an adventure, and their reputation as one of the universe's mightiest races has won them respect and dread from other people. Their contacts with humanity over 1,000 years ago had a significant impact on Scandinavian culture, with the Asgardians serving as the model for Norse mythology in the area.

The Asgardians' population has plummeted in the aftermath of Ragnarök, the Attack on the Statesman, and the Snap, with most of them being killed. In 2023, however, Hulk used the Infinity Stones to resurrect the Snap victims.

Malekith, the ruler of the Dark Elves, initiated a mission to restore the cosmos to its original condition of darkness using an Infinity Stone called the Aether over 5,000 years ago, during the time of the Convergence of the Nine

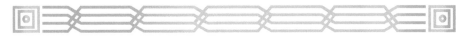

Realms. Under the leadership of their monarch, Bor, the Asgardians stood in his way.

The Asgardians defeated the Dark Elves and claimed the Aether before Malekith could utilize its power. Malekith, his lieutenant Algrim, and a force of Dark Elf soldiers fled the last fight and entered a state of long sleep, planning to awaken at the next Convergence and resume their ambitions for global conquest.

6.1 Conquering the Nine Realms

Odin and Hela conquer other kingdoms.

Bor was followed by his son Odin, who led Asgard in a brutal conquest, bringing all of the Nine Realms under Asgard's control, with his daughter and Executioner Hela at his side. Hela's goals, however, went beyond the borders of Yggdrasil, and she started scheming a more extensive and bloodier invasion of other planets.

Odin, seeing the consequences of his warlike worldview for the first time and unable to reason with his daughter, exiled her to Hel. Odin then removed all references to his despotic daughter from Asgardian art and records, assuring her oblivion throughout history.

Odin sent his Valkyries to Hel to murder her so that Hela would not return. On the other hand, Hela defeated the warriors and killed everyone except Valkyrie.

The Asgardians mingled with individuals of all races and civilizations as a technologically sophisticated, spacefaring species. The Kree, Centaurians, Korbinites, Badoon, and the Nova Empire, as well as Knowhere, were among those known. Interdites, Sarks, Centaurians, Levians, Pheragots, Kree, and Jotuns are among the blue aliens Sif has encountered. The Asgardians gained a better reputation due to their contacts with other cosmic groupings, garnering

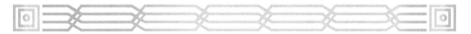

respect from various species and creating enemies of others. Asgardians were educated about the other races as youngsters, including learning their languages.

Although they have interacted with societies from other planets, Asgardians do not have particularly deep relationships with cultures from beyond the Nine Realms. They are not regarded as major members of the integrated space society despite their existence. Lady Sif incorrectly told Phil Coulson that the Frost Giants were the only blue-skinned extraterrestrial species, while the Kree had visited Earth long before Odin's rule. Another example is when Thor informs the Avengers that the Chitauri are not from any known world, despite their living in the Sanctuary area of space. Thor had previously talked with Loki, the Chitauri's former leader, who informed him that he had learned many things during his exile, including planets that Thor and the rest of the Asgardians are unaware of, like the Chitauri space.

6.2 Traveling to Earth

The Frost Giants of Jotunheim began their conquest of the Nine Realms in 965 AD, beginning with Earth. The Asgardians, now ruled by Bor's son Odin, came to save humanity. The Asgardians eventually drove the Frost Giants back to Jotunheim, where Odin personally defeated Laufey, the Jotun king, until he surrendered. The Asgardians seized the Casket of Ancient Winters, Jotunheim's greatest weapon, and carried it back to Asgard for safety once the ceasefire was reached.

Odin discovered Laufey's abandoned kid in Jotunheim and chose to raise him alongside his son, Thor. Odin gave the infant the name Loki and intended to bring the two realms together and establish a lasting peace.

The Berserker Force, an Asgardian army, arrived in Midgard in the 12th century. They were primarily or entirely made up of Asgardian people who had volunteered for the expedition but were not fighters. They gained considerably increased strength and an intense feeling of fury by touching the

Berserker Staff. Except for one, The Warrior Who Stayed, later known as Elliot Randolph, who'd already fallen in love with Earth and its culture. The army returned to Asgard once the battle ended. He shattered the Berserker Staff into three pieces and dispersed them throughout Europe while concealing his true identity. However, in the 1500s, he repeated his story to a French girl, whose brother, a priest, recorded it, and the legend of the Berserkers was born.

Asgardians started to visit Earth, and they developed a deep bond with the humans. With Odin, Thor and Loki paid a visit to Earth. The Asgardians taught the Norse people their language and culture while also demonstrating their talents, leading them to assume the Asgardians were gods and bestowing the titles "God of Thunder" and "God of Mischief" on Thor and Loki, respectively. This custom was carried on for many years. Odin took the Tesseract from his vault and carried it to Tnsberg, Norway, where he left it in the hands of ardent Asgardian devotees on one of these journeys.

6.3 Thor's Banishment

Thor had shown himself to be a worthy prince six millennia later, protecting Asgard in several conflicts and gaining a reputation as a hero. When Odin eventually proclaimed Thor king, a jealous Loki postponed the ceremony. Loki permitted three Frost Giants to infiltrate Asgard via a hidden conduit into Jotunheim, where they sought to take their Casket from Odin's Trophy Room. Thor's coronation was postponed despite the unsuccessful attempt. Thor, Loki, Sif, and the Warriors Three, filled with fury, traveled to Jotunheim and started murdering as many Frost Giants as they could.

When Odin tried to settle things down, Laufey proclaimed they were at war again. Odin took Thor's hammer, Mjolnir, and exiled him to Earth to learn humility and show himself worthy of the kingship when he returned to Asgard. Loki confronted Odin about his origins and learned how he was discovered. Odin went into the Odinsleep under extreme stress, allowing Loki to ascend to the throne.

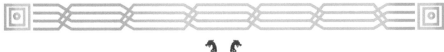

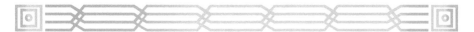

Loki devised a scheme and traveled to Earth, telling Thor that he must stay in exile on Earth since Odin had died because of the prospect of a new battle. Loki then traveled to Jotunheim and made a pact with Laufey, allowing him to enter Asgard and murder Odin as he slept. Meanwhile, Sif and the Warriors Three had journeyed to Earth to reunite with Thor. Loki had sent the Destroyer to pursue them. Thor showed himself worthy in a brutal fight in a little hamlet, and his abilities were restored, resulting in the Destroyer's defeat. After the catastrophe, the Earth began to believe in tales once again.

When Laufey sought to make the death stroke against Odin back in Asgard, Loki betrayed him and slaughtered him. Thor quickly went to Asgard and met Loki, who revealed his plan to destroy Jotunheim using the Bifrost to show his value to Odin.

6.4 The Bridge Destroyed

Thor was obliged to demolish the Rainbow Bridge and rescue Jotunheim during the brothers' Duel at the Rainbow Bridge. Odin awakened from his slumber, but he refused Loki's invitation to join him. Loki then let himself fall into the infinite void of space. The Asgardians praised Thor's homecoming and heroism, but they faced a larger challenge. Asgard would be unable to safeguard the Nine Realms without the Bifrost.

Sensing Asgard's absence, a ragged band of invaders called the Marauders set out to plunder and slaughter their way through the realms. Meanwhile, Asgard realized Loki was still alive and had struck a pact with Thanos, the extraterrestrial despot. Loki has come to Earth to reclaim the Tesseract in exchange for leadership of the Chitauri army and the right to govern the world. Odin sent Thor to Earth to fetch Loki and the Tesseract home using dark energy.

6.5 Loki's War on Earth

Loki arrived on Earth via the Tesseract and went about spreading havoc to declare himself Earth's ruler. Loki used mind control to have numerous humans construct a device that would enable the Chitauri to attack Earth by harnessing the Tesseract's power and opening a gateway.

Loki and his army were greeted with combat as they lay waste to New York City, coming into confrontation with S.H.I.E.L.D., the Avengers, and Thor. Thor used the Tesseract to return Loki to Asgard for punishment after the Chitauri were defeated and the gateway closed.

6.6 War of the Realms

When Heimdall returned to Asgard, he used the Tesseract to resurrect the Bifrost. Meanwhile, Loki was imprisoned for his activities on Asgard, Jotunheim, and Earth, and Thor was sent to lead Asgardian warriors against the

Marauders, who were still spreading devastation throughout the Nine Realms and beyond to worlds like Harokin, Nix, Korbin, and Ria.

After a two-year conflict, all of the Marauders were apprehended and imprisoned on Asgard, and the Realms were at peace once again, owing to their tranquility to Asgard. Odin, pleased with the man his son had grown into, decided it was time to crown Thor king, something he had become afraid of after years of combat.

6.7 The Dark Elves Return

The Dark Elves awakened five thousand years after their species had been destroyed, the moment of the Convergence approaching once again. Meanwhile, Jane Foster was transported to where the Aether was concealed after coming across portals left by the Convergence on Earth. Foster became the reluctant host of the Aether after releasing it. Thor traveled to Earth to find his companion, with whom he had built a loving bond during his two-year exile on Earth and brought her to Asgard for safety.

Malekith developed a ruse in which he disguised his henchman Algrim as a Marauder and imprisoned him in Asgard. Algrim used the Kursed's power to change himself into an invincible beast within the dungeons. Algrim broke Asgard's defenses by releasing the Marauders from their prisons, enabling the Dark Elves to conquer Asgard. During the commotion, several captives escaped from their cells, including Lorelei, who made her way down to Midgard.

As the battle between the two sides began, the Asgardians and Dark Elves lost ground. Malekith had Algrim kill Queen Frigga before departing on their ship since he couldn't find Aether's host. Asgard lamented Frigga and their dead. Odin, distraught by the death of his wife, ordered the Bifrost to be turned off and all Asgardians to be grounded in preparation for Malekith's retaliation.

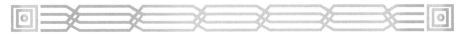

Thor, seeking vengeance, liberated Loki from his jail and fled from Asgard with Foster with the assistance of Sif and the Warriors Three. They transported to the Dark Elves' homeworld, Svartalfheim, via a spatial fissure discovered by Loki many years before. Despite Thor and Loki's greatest attempts to destroy it, Malekith was able to take the Aether from Foster's body. Thor and Foster were stuck on Svartalfheim when Loki sacrificed himself to destroy Algrim, while Malekith traveled to Earth to release the Aether at the Convergence's conclusion. Thor faced Malekith and killed him with the assistance of Foster, Erik Selvig, Darcy Lewis, and Ian Boothby, returning to the same London warehouse from which Foster and Thor had left Earth.

6.8 Immigration on Earth

After Loki's invasion, S.H.I.E.L.D. has become warier of supernatural dangers on Earth. The CIA discovered that several Asgardians had made Earth their home in their attempts to maintain world peace and repel potential threats. Elliot Randolph and the sorceress Lorelei were two notable examples. The former helped S.H.I.E.L.D. stop a Norse hate organization from utilizing an Asgardian weapon, the Berserker Staff, for evil purposes. The latter became an adversary of S.H.I.E.L.D., who joined up with Sif to defeat her.

Meanwhile, Asgardians served as guardians of the Nine Realms' planets. Sif was sent to Earth when Heimdall spotted a Kree. She eventually took him back to Asgard before he departed for Hala.

Thor linked up with the Avengers once again to hunt down the Chitauri scepter held by HYDRA and battle Ultron, artificial intelligence built from the Scepter's alien supercomputer that had gone genocidal. Thor and Erik Selvig traveled to the Water of Sights to learn more about the Infinity Stones after receiving visions from the Scarlet Witch that promised calamity on Asgard. Thor then returned to Asgard.

Elliot Randolph joined with S.H.I.E.L.D. once again to discover how to utilize and then destroy the Monolith, an ancient Kree gateway. Fearful of being pulled back through a portal to Asgard or somewhere else, Randolph volunteered to assist S.H.I.E.L.D. understand how the gateway operated in return for the portal being destroyed.

From the Lighthouse, the Chronicon Noah kept an eye out for extinction-level occurrences. An Asgardian who was observed in a city was one of his discoveries.

After two years of quest for the Infinity Stones, Thor returns to Asgard. He realized that Loki was still alive and ruling Asgard under the guise of Odin. They flew to Earth and discovered a dying Odin in Norway with the assistance of Doctor Strange. Odin informed his sons before he died that their sister, Hela, would be free and attempt to control Asgard by force. Hela stood before them after Odin's death, claiming to be their queen and destroying Mjolnir. Skurge transferred the three across the Bifrost Bridge, but Hela tossed the two out, and they landed on Sakaar's world.

Hela instantly challenged the Einherjar to a battle, killing the soldiers and the Warriors Three in the process. She selected Skurge as her executioner and reigned terror over the Asgardians. On the other hand, Heimdall escorted the Asgardian citizens to a haven where they might hide from Hela. Meanwhile, in Sakaar, Thor reconnected with the Hulk and, together with Valkyrie, departed the planet and traveled to Asgard. At the same time, Loki joined the Sakaaran Rebellion and traveled to Asgard.

While the rest of the Avengers and Asgardians attacked Hela's army of Berserkers, Thor challenged her to a fight. When Loki joined the battle and assisted in the evacuation of the Asgardians from Asgard aboard a Sakaaran ship, Thor urged Loki to fuse the Crown of Surtur with the Eternal Flame, causing Surtur to trigger the Ragnarök to murder Hela. Although the strategy worked, the Asgardians were left without a homeworld. Thor, their new monarch, set sail towards Earth in search of safety.

6.9 Brink of Extinction

Thanos and the Black Order intercepted the Statesman. Half of the Asgardians that survived were slain in the ensuing battle. Valkyrie was spared and permitted to flee with half of the Asgardians in escape pods. Thor,

Heimdall, and Loki were the only ones who survived the battle. On the other hand, Heimdall was murdered when he used the last of his energy to transfer the Hulk to Earth through the Bifrost. Loki was slain shortly after trying to slay Thanos. The Asgardian population was once again half after the Snap.

Together with Valkyrie, Korg, and Miek, the surviving Asgardians reestablished civilization on Earth in Tnsberg, Norway, which they dubbed New Asgard. The Asgardians were stripped of their wealth and forced to live a modest, rural existence, with many becoming fishers. They were headed by Thor, although they didn't see him until he needed more booze due to his hermetic drinking and video gaming lifestyle. Hulk and Rocket Raccoon paid a visit to New Asgard in 2023, bringing Thor with them.

6.10 Earth's Battle

The Asgardian population was restored once the Blip was enforced. Shortly after, the Masters of the Mystic Arts dispatched Valkyrie, the Einherjar, Korg, and Miek through a portal to combat alternative Thanos and his army in the devastated Avengers Compound.

6.11 Alternative Universes

Asgardians are a technologically superior warrior species with technology beyond human understanding. Some Asgardian gadgets have cryptic, ancient-sounding names that make them seem archaic. Asgardians are a warlike nation, and the Nine Realms have been peaceful for millennia thanks to Asgard's army. They have energy weapons and planes that look like Viking longboats but are equipped with guns and missiles. An energy barrier shields the royal palace, and the Bifrost, a world-spanning bridge, allows transit between the Nine Realms. Asgardians have complex password systems that can even be etched in stone to enter doors. The Destroyer, for example, is a gadget that combines modern technology with magic.

Regular melee weapons, such as swords, spears, and shields, are used by Asgardian soldiers. These weapons, on the other hand, are constructed of cutting-edge technology. When moving quickly (e.g., sword slashing in battle), the blade glows with a bluish-white aura of energy, greatly increasing the weapon's power (a strange vibration is often audible while the individual handles the weapon, indicating that the blade can turn blue at any time), rendering handheld weapons obsolete: be they lightning, bullets, or arrows. Similarly, when some Asgardian weapons hit, they may produce hot blue or orange sparks; likewise, they produce similar sparks when an Asgardian armor is struck. Asgardian shields may deflect laser blasts; when a blast strikes the shield, it ripples with the same energy and deflects the blast. Another Asgardian technology has the same energy. It is created as a shield to defend the palace and is shot by cannons.

The Rainbow Bridge, which is capable of harnessing and producing a Bifrost Bridge, is one of the Asgardians' most essential pieces of technology. Heimdall controls the Bifrost and looks over the Nine Realms and space from Himinbjorg, linked to Asgard by the Rainbow Bridge. The Asgardians may travel to other worlds via the Bifrost instead of spacecraft, as other societies do.

6.12 Characteristic Traits

While Asgardians and humans seem to be the same, they are very different, having various superhuman skills. One of their most important powers is a varying degree of superhuman strength. The ordinary Asgardian is powerful enough to take on any entity from the Nine Realms. More evolved fighters like Heimdall, the Warriors Three, Frigga, Sif, and the Valkyrie have more strength, allowing them to easily defeat low-level Asgardian warriors (or, in Frigga's case, combat a Dark Elf to a surprising degree). Due to his time as a Berserker, Elliot Randolph may still retain a degree of power that puts him in the same category. Bor, Odin, Hela, and Thor, Asgard's royal family members, seem to be the most powerful Asgardians. As Hela was defeated by her father Odin, and Thor even admitted that his father was stronger than him, whoever is now the crowned monarch of Asgard may be granted some strength.

Thor was able to confront a raging Hulk before he could hit Black Widow, and Asgardians also have superhuman speed, agility, reflexes, and coordination (as seen by Thor ducking the wing of a S.H.I.E.L.D. jet aircraft that was launched at him).

Most importantly, Asgardians are very durable and regenerate quickly. As with their strength, Asgardian endurance varies from individual to individual. Even though the ordinary Asgardian can withstand the most formidable opponents, they are nevertheless vulnerable to death. Warriors with highly developed endurance, such as Heimdall, the Warriors Three, and Sif, can hold their own against mighty opponents like the Destroyer. The royal family, yet again, is the most resilient.

Even while Asgardians can withstand much more unusual physical punishment than a typical human, they are susceptible to injury. Their regeneration powers are activated at this stage. They can recover far quicker than humans because of their talents. On Asgard, however, there is a "healing chamber" that assists in hastening the treatment of severe injuries among the common populace. Odin seems to be one of the few Asgardians immune to such safeguards, instead opting for the Odinsleep, a prolonged time of sus

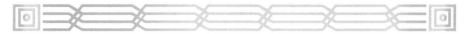

pended animation during which he regenerates his power. Thor's regeneration powers are superior to those of the normal Asgardian, considering he is Odin's son. To have the same effect on an Asgardian as a human, alcohol must be stronger or consumed in larger amounts. Thor drank a thousand-year-old alcoholic beverage to experience the effects, while Elliot Randolph got inebriated after eating an enormous quantity.

The regenerative powers of Asgardians allow them to live longer lives. Even though humanity believes them to be immortal, Odin has said they are not. Even while they are not immortal, Asgardians live significantly longer, "give or take 5,000 years," according to Loki. By the Second Dark Elf Battle, Odin's father Bor, for example, is long dead, having lived his 5,000 years sometime after the first conflict. Asgardians mature like humans for the first 20 years or so of their lives. They begin to mature considerably more slowly as they reach early adulthood.

The internal anatomy of Asgardians differs from that of humans, having denser bones, tissue, and skin. Human physicians are unfamiliar with Asgardian anatomy and lack the requisite skills to heal an injured Asgardian, despite having red blood like humans. While Earthly materials may harm them if held by someone with superhuman strength or sophisticated technology, the strength and technology of the typical person are insufficient to do so.

Asgardians with powerful magical skills have been revealed to disintegrate into energy at the moment of death, as Odin and Hela did, or after an elaborate burial rite, as Frigga did.

Other Asgardians merely bury their dead; Hela's zombie soldiers might be resurrected after millennia of imprisonment.

The Asgardians are warriors, and they thirst to fighting since children. They have been trained in the use of numerous weapons and hand-to-hand warfare; Queen Frigga was able to go toe-to-toe with Malekith, defeating him in sword battle. Many Asgardian people also armed themselves to aid in the struggle against Hela's zombie army. They are also educated about the races

of the Nine Realms and beyond as youngsters, even acquiring the languages of other races.

The Asgardians use a writing system akin to the Nordic runes used on Earth, and their spoken language is comparable to Norwegian. In Asgardian society, fathers are supposedly revered by having their offspring called after them, with names written similarly to Icelandic surnames (examples being Thor Odinson and Sylvie Laufeydottir). It's likely that Asgardians passed on their written and spoken linguistic skills to the ancient Scandinavians with whom they interacted, inspiring the development of their languages.

Chapter 7

HOW NORSE MYTHOLOGY INFLUENCED MODERN POP CULTURE

Chapter 7: How Norse Mythology Influenced Modern Pop Culture

There has been a spike in interest in Norse mythology in popular culture in recent years, with the ancient stories inspiring novels, games, films, and television series. But how did ancient tales manage to have such a huge impact on popular culture? Let's have a look at what we've got.

7.1 Film and Television

There have been scores of films and television series loosely based on Norse mythology or media that have given the traditional narratives a contemporary or distinctive spin. The Marvel Cinematic Universe, on which Thor, Odin, Loki, Asgard, and many other pieces of old mythical stories are based, is perhaps one of the most modern and largest interpretations of Nose mythology.

These films are based on Marvel's Thor comics and served as many people's first exposure to Norse mythology, notably English novelist Neil Gaiman, who wrote the Norse mythological-inspired book American Gods.

7.2 Video and Casino Games

There has also been an increase in the number of games based on Norse mythology in recent years. Sony PlayStation's God Of War, Microsoft's Hellblade: Senua's Sacrifice, and Control are three notable video games based on Norse mythology. God Of War, in particular, is influenced by Norse mythology since it includes allusions to Loki and Jörmungandr the Midgard Serpent, as well as having players travel to many of the nine Norse realms through Yggdrasil as Ragnarök approaches.

7.3 Books

Norse mythology's impact may also be seen in George R. R. Martin's critically hailed Game of Thrones series, which has Direwolves (Wolves that often figured in Norse mythology), White Walkers (Ice Giants), and Ravens, who served as god Odin's familiars.

Many other stories, such as Joanne M. Harris' Runemarks, in which the protagonist is summoned by a stranger known as One-Eye, and even many of the Witcher books, are influenced by Norse mythology.
You can see how Norse mythology has affected popular culture today, and its appeal is undeniable. While most of the media mentioned above do not provide real or exact adaptations of the original mythological stories, they are a fun way to pass the time. They may serve as an excellent introduction to myths that have yet to be adapted or narrated.

7.4 Animation

He-Man, the famous 1980s cartoon, takes many elements from Norse mythology, such as respecting the dead, using magical weapons, and celebrating fights and wins. Snow White and the Seven Dwarfs, a Disney animated film based on the Brothers Grimm fairytale, are based on the ancient Norse legend of the goddess Freyja seeking assistance from the dwarfs.

7.5 Comics

This is maybe the most straightforward example since numerous comic books have been created portraying Vikings, Norse mythology, and other topics. Thor, the Marvel comic book superhero, is based on Norse mythology. Death Wish Coffee Presents: Odinforce — our comic series — is the greatest representation of Vikings in comic books.

Odin

Odin, Thor's father, is also known as "all-father" in Old Norse mythology; he is the eldest of the gods and the originator of life. Odin reigns from Asgard, the land of the gods, despite being blind in one eye (which he exchanged for infinite knowledge). Huginn and Muninn, his two ravens, accompany him across the globe and tell him everything. Odin, the god of battle, rejoices in the heroic deaths of warriors, whom he subsequently takes into Valhalla, the realm of the brave. He is cruel and vengeful, but he is not unjust.

In popular culture, Odin originally appeared in the same Marvel issue as Thor in 1962 and has since been a regular figure. He was presented as a member of an old Avengers squad in one of the most recent seasons (like his son is part of the current one). In the Marvel cinematic world, Odin has been depicted on the big screen by Anthony Hopkins, although many of the character's ethically murky elements have been hushed up. American Gods, starring Ian McShane as the intriguing Mr. Wednesday, gives a significantly more fascinating picture of Odin (Wednesday is the day traditionally dedicated to Odin).

Thor

According to Old Norse mythology, he is tall, muscular, and red-bearded, the god of thunder may not be as brilliant as his father (or Loki), but he has a kind heart. His Megingjord belt amplifies his strength, and he wields Mjolnir, the magical hammer that can change the size and always returns to him. He is the guardian of both Asgard, the realm of the gods, as Midgard, the land of mortals, and is married to golden-haired Sif.

In pop culture, he made his Marvel début in 1962 and was a founding member of the superhero team in the inaugural issue of Avengers in 1963. Since then, he's been featured in a slew of comic books, animated series, and video games, but Chris Hemsworth's depiction of Asgardian (2011) and Avengers: Infinity War cemented the character's popularity (2018).

Freya/Frigg

Freya, along with her twin brother Frey, is a member of the Vanir, a race of nature gods who were assigned to dwell among the gods of Asgard as part of peace after battling with them. Freya, the goddess of love and most beautiful of them all, was the most beautiful. Everyone wanted to marry her or kidnap her at some point (or both). She possessed a cat-drawn flying chariot and a penchant for the high life; Loki once accused her of having affairs with many gods. Freya is often confused with Frigg, Odin's wife, and gods' queen.

Frigga originally debuted as Thor's mother (and Loki's adoptive mother) in Marvel comics in 1963, while a distinct character called Freya had a brief cameo in 1993. After 2011, both characters were treated as though they were the same person. Frigga was played by Rene Russo in the first two Thor films.

Loki

In Old Norse mythology, you'll probably meet a distinct version of Loki depending on the manuscript/branch of Norse mythology you read.

Nobody appears to agree on the nature of Loki's kinship with Odin (some suggest blood siblings), but it is widely assumed that his father was a giant. While living in Asgard with the other gods, Loki never appears to feel like an equal, and it's never clear whose side of a dispute he'll choose. Loki, a crafty shape-shifter with flying shoes, enjoys pranking Thor and is known as "The Trickster."

In pop culture, Marvel's version of Loki initially appears in the 1962 issue as Thor's step-brother and arch-enemy—he's considered one of the best comic book villains of all time. Tom Hiddleston originally played Loki in the Marvel Cinematic Universe in 2011 and has since produced a wickedly colorful portrayal. Outside of Marvel, Loki appears in The CW's Supernatural as a recurring character, played by Richard Speight Jr. Although this Loki is less flashy and grungier, it remains loyal to the Norse stories' Trickster essence.

Hel

Hel is Loki's proscribed daughter with a giantess, and one of the reasons Loki is known as the "Father of Monsters" in Old Norse mythology. Odin gives her charge of the dead land (those who were not accepted in Valhalla)

since she is a half gorgeous girl and half decaying corpse. After her, the realm was termed Hel, and it is thought that the Christian term "hell" is derived from a later variation of the same word.

In contemporary culture, the figure is Hela in Marvel comics, and she originally debuted in the 1964 issue as Loki's daughter, closely matching the original plot. However, Cate Blanchett's role in Thor: Ragnarok (2017) is Odin's first-born child, fighting Thor for possession of Asgard. Although pop culture does not always adhere to the original mythology, it helps to keep the tales alive.

Chapter 8

THE END
TIME

Chapter 8: The End Time

The end of the world has been fermenting for roughly 100 days, according to Norse mythology. It all began when Loki's wolf son escaped from jail, and the massive Midgard Serpent sprang from the sea.

Ragnarok will climax in an epic fight on Saturday. Thor, Loki, Odin, Freyr, Hermór, and all the other Norse gods will battle, the Earth will tumble into the sea, and existence as we know it will come to an end.

Ragnarok has had a wide cultural impact, inspiring anything from 13th-century Eddic poetry to the last part of Wagner's Ring Cycle to death metal. But none of it matters now as the world is coming to an end in a week.

Vikings are already assembling in York, England, to spend their last days on Earth for the JORVIK Viking Festival. A procession, a staged fight, a light display, and fireworks will usher in Ragnarok.

Let's take a peek at the Norse mythical realm before we get into the devastating events of Ragnarök. It consisted of nine planets, one of which was Asgard, home of the sir god clan. The Vanir, a pantheon of gods that dwelt in

Vanaheim, was gods' second pantheon. According to folklore, the nine worlds encircled and stretched out from the Yggdrasil, a holy cosmic tree at the center of the cosmos.

In today's world, the sir had the most well-known names of the two primary groups of gods. Odin, Thor, Frigg, Balder, Heimdall, Hör, and Tyr made up the pantheon, while the Vanir held Njörr, Freyr, Freya, Gullveig, and Nerthus. When it comes to understanding Ragnarök, it's crucial to remember that Loki, the legendary trickster god, was neither sir nor Vanir. Even though the gods of the two pantheons were often at odds in Norse mythology, the events of Ragnarök had nothing to do with their continuous rivalry.

So, how will it all come to an end? Several indications will announce the arrival of Ragnarök's prophesy. The first is the arrival of the Fimbulwinter ('big winter,') which would see the earth ravaged by three consecutive winters with no summers in between. The hard winter will deliver an infinite supply of snow from all directions, depleting food and supplies. As the winter destroys the fields and the shreds of what's left are fought for tooth and nail, humanity will descend into a world of violence. It is predicted that brothers murder brothers, dads kill sons, and natural family relationships will be shattered as the simple drive to live plagues everyone.

The wolves Skoll and Hati have been chasing the sun and moon since the beginning of time. They ultimately grab their victim during Ragnarök. The sky darkens, the stars vanish, and the ground violently trembles as a result. Mountains will be destroyed, forests will be overturned, and the wolf Fenrir will be freed from his shackles. Fenrir is Loki's offspring which the other gods enslaved because he was foretold to do them great harm.

During this time, another Loki kid will appear on the scene. As the seas flood onto the land, Jörmungandr, the sea serpent of Midgard (the realm of humanity), will break it. Naglfar, a ship fashioned entirely of human fingernails and toenails stolen from the bodies of deceased men and women, will break away from its mooring. The ship will be brimming with an army of giants that will navigate the flooded land with ease. Hrymr, a frost-giant, will be at the helm.

Fenrir will go wild with his eyes and nostrils blazing, opening his mouth so wide that his top jaw touches the sky and his bottom one gouges through the ground. Jörmungandr will spew venom all over the place, poisoning everything in his path.

The dome of the sky will break apart, and fire-giants from the realm of Muspelheim will spring out from the opening as the two monsters run amok. Surtr, wielding a blazing sword reputed to be brighter than the sun, will lead them. The fire-giants will cross the Bifröst, the rainbow bridge that connects man's realm with Asgard. The bridge will collapse behind them as they cross it. They'll next go to the huge expanses of Vgrr's field.

Fenrir, Jörmungandr, Hrymr, and Loki will join them on the vast battleground. Loki had previously been imprisoned in a cave by the other gods for his role in Balder's death. He will be able to break free from his bonds and join the others in Vgrr to battle the sir gods thanks to the events of Ragnarök.

Heimdall, the god's watchman and guardian of the Bifröst bridge, will sound the Gjallarhorn, his great horn. The boom will be heard across all worlds, awaking the gods who will realize the end of the world has arrived. As Odin descends under Yggdrasil in pursuit of advice from Mmir, the wisest of all creatures, Yggdrasil will begin to tremble.

A Vanir deity kept prisoner by the sir following the Sir-Vanir War, Freyr will be among them. He is the only deity of the Vanir tribe referenced in ancient poetry as participating in the battle.

Odin will ride towards Fenrir as the battle begins, while Thor will fight Jörmungandr. Odin will be encased in golden armor from head to toe, carrying his legendary Gungrir spear. The einherjar, selected men who perished in combat and were carried to Valhalla's grand hall to prepare for Ragnarök, will be by his side. Odin and his band of human warriors will face off against Fenrir, fighting with bravery that the world has never seen before.

The prophecies, however, have predicted their demise, and Fenrir will engulf them all, even the "father of the gods." His triumph will be short-lived, as Odin's son Varr seeks vengeance for his father's murder by pulling the

huge wolf's jaws apart and stabbing it through the neck, quickly killing him. When Thor and Jörmungandr fight, the Jörmungandr will show to be a worthy opponent. Thor's powerful hammer, the Mjolnir, will slam the serpent to the ground. The triumph, however, will be his last. The serpent's venom will poison Thor throughout the battle, and he will stumble for just nine steps after slaughtering the beast before dropping dead.

Surtr will slay Freyr, and Tyr will be murdered by Garmr, another wolf of the underworld, during the fight. Loki's naughty pranks will come to a stop on the Vgrr battlefield when he and Heimdall extinguish one other's life.

Surtr will consume the earth in flames as the bloody fight concludes, causing everything to burn. The flames will ascend to the skies as the land collapses into the sea.

The flames will eventually go out, and the earth will emerge from the ocean. A fish-hunting eagle will soar over a mountain's gushing waterfall. After the events of Ragnarök, the male gods Hör and Balder, who had previously died and gone to Hel, are revived. After the Sir-Vanir War, the Vanir deity Njörr, another Sir prisoner, is said to return 'home among the wise Vanir.' The sons of Odin and Thor will also survive; the former will live in the gods' temple, while the latter will continue to wield the legendary Mjolnir. As a result, it seems that not all gods will perish during Ragnarök.

Ragnarok (Old Norse Ragnarök) was the Vikings' name for the day when they thought the world as we know it would come to an end. Ragnarok is the end of the Gods and Goddesses and the end of humanity. The last battle between the Aesir and the Giants will take place. The fight will take place in the Vigrid plains.

The giant Midgard snake will emerge from the water here, splashing its tail and spraying poison in all directions, causing massive waves to smash on the shore. Surtr, the fire giant, will set fire to Asgard (the abode of the Gods and Goddesses) and the rainbow bridge Bifrost in the meanwhile. The Fenrir wolf will break free from his shackles and wreak havoc on the world. The wolves Sköll and Hati will consume the sun and moon, and the world tree Yggdrasil will shake the earth.

Thor will defeat the Midgard Serpent and slay it, but he will die due to the Midgard Serpent's deadly wounds. Surtr, a fire giant, will assassinate Freyr. Surtr will finally set fire to all nine planets, causing everything to plunge into the boiling sea. Ragnarok will happen regardless of what the gods do. Odin's sole solace is knowing that Ragnarok will not bring the end of the world.

There will be certain warning signs if Ragnarok, "the end of the world" is approaching. The first indication is the assassination of God Baldr, Odin's and Frigg's son, which has already occurred.

The second warning will be three consecutive long, frigid winters, each lasting three years and with no summer in between. Throughout these three long years, Battles will afflict the globe, and brothers will slaughter brothers since the word for these unbroken winters is "Fimbulwinter." Two wolves will swallow the sun and moon in the sky, and even the stars will vanish, leaving the planet in complete darkness.

Fjalar, a gorgeous red rooster whose name means "All-Knower," will alert all of the giants that Ragnarok has started. A crimson rooster will tell all the dishonorable dead in Hel that the conflict has started at the same moment. A red rooster named "Gullinkambi" will also alert all the Gods in Asgard.

Heimdall will blast his horn as loudly as he can, signaling the beginning of the conflict to all the einherjar in Valhalla. This will be the battle to end all battles and the day when all the "Einherjar" from Valhalla and Folkvangr who have died honorably in combat will take up their swords and armor to fight with the Aesir against the Giants.

The Gods, Baldr, and Hod will rise from the dead to battle with their brothers and sisters one more time. Odin will ride his horse Sleipnir to the fight in the fields of Vigrid, wearing his eagle helmet and wielding his spear Gungnir, and leading Asgard's massive army of Gods and courageous einherjar.

The Giants, together with Hel and all her shameful dead, will travel to the plains of Vigrid aboard the ship Naglfar, which is built of all the dead's

fingernails. Nidhogg, the dragon, will soar throughout the battlefield, gathering as many bodies as he can for his never-ending thirst.

Several Gods will live, including Odin's sons Vidar and Vali and his brother Honor. Modi and Magni, Thor's sons, will inherit Mjolnir, their father's hammer.

The few Gods who survive will go to Idavoll, spared from destruction. And there will be new homes built here, the most important of which will be Gimli, which will have a gold roof. There's also a new area named Brimir, located in Okolnir, which means "never cold." It's in the Nidafjoll mountains.

However, there is a dreadful spot on Nastrond, a big hall on the coast of corpses. All of the doors face north, greeting the howling winds. Snakes will writhe on the walls, releasing their poison into a river that runs through the hall. This will be the new underworld, full of thieves and murderers, and when they die, the big dragon Nidogg will be there to devour their bodies.

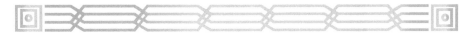

Conclusion

The Vikings found Norse Mythology to be a highly fascinating religion. It kept people upbeat during difficult times. There were a lot of gods and a lot of tales. The religion of Norse Mythology was well-developed. Everything was a barrel of fun, or a renewing war cry to the Vikings, from Valhalla to the gods of Aesir!

During the Dark Ages, Teutonic religion spread over Scandinavia, Germany, and England, but the ancient gods and ceremonies were destroyed and forgotten. The Elder Edda and the Younger Edda, which were collected in Iceland during the Middle Ages, provide us with a great deal of information on this religion. The Eddas provide a bleak picture of the universe and man's place in it.

The universe began when Odin and his brothers slew the primordial Frost-Giant Ymir, and it will end when the Giants rise against Odin and his companions and slaughter them in battle. The gods and humans alike face certain destruction. Still, the only honorable activity in the face of that dread is combat, and dying valiantly fighting was the only way to join Valhalla, the warrior's heaven. In Norse mythology, love was often accompanied by violent impulses, and betrayal was prevalent. The world is a harsh, cold, and terrible place to live.

Odin (Woden, Wotan) was the supreme deity of the Norse gods, a master of intellect, magic, and poetry. He was the deity of the fallen and the defender of brave noblemen in battle. Odin was blind in one eye, wore golden armor and helmet, wielded a magical spear, and rode Sleipnir, a lightning-fast eight-legged horse. Hugin and Munin (thinking and memory), two ravens perched on his shoulders, flew over the earth and reported back to him each night.

Odin's wife, Frigga, was a smart woman. She defended courageous soldiers who Odin overlooked. Frigga and Odin were both involved in extramarital affairs.

Thor was the god of thunder, a mighty deity with a good nature but a fearsome reputation among his foes. He defended peasant warriors with a belt that increased his strength, iron gloves, and Mjolnir, a magical hammer that always hit its target and returned to Thor's hand.

Balder, the son of Odin and Frigga, was particularly liked and adored by practically everyone on the planet, yet he was the first deity to die, assassinated by Loki's treachery.

Tyr was in charge of public gatherings, legal proceedings, and warfare. Fenrir the wolf, a fearsome adversary of the gods, chewed off his hand.

Frey was the deity of fertility and greenery.

His sister, Freya, was a goddess of love and beauty.

Heimdall was the gods' watchman, stationed on Bifrost, the rainbow bridge that led to Asgard. His trumpet would sound like the end of the world.

Although Loki was permitted in Asgard, he was the son of a Giant. He was full of malice and cunning, and he wreaked havoc until the gods imprisoned him in a hole and tormented him with a poisonous snake. Fenrir the wolf and the Midgard Serpent are two of his three great creatures.

Hel, the goddess of the netherworld, had human characteristics on half of her face and was blank on the other. She was the Queen of the Dead.

NORSE PAGANISM

A Complete Guide for You to Understand
the Values, Realms, and Myths of Norse
Paganism

Introduction

During the Proto-Norse era, when the Germanic peoples separated into their group, the Old Norse religion, also known as Norse mythology, became the most famous term for a stream of German religion that formed. In the process of Christianization in Scandinavia, it was displaced by Christianity and eventually forgotten. To reconstruct components of North Germanic religion, intellectuals use chronological discourse analysis, archaeological sites, toponymy, and documentation retained by North Germanic tribes, including such Cyrillic manuscripts within Younger Ancient runes, a distinctively Germanic enhanced version of the runic alphabet, as well as other sources.

As an aspect of Germanic religion, Norse mythology has been recorded in various pieces of Old Norse literature going back to the 13th century. Many people today are acquainted with the religious figures and legends of the Nordic tribes, those groupings of people who lived in present-day Scandinavia during the time of the Vikings. Norse mythology, on the other hand, is more than simply a collection of tales and intriguing people with supernatural abilities. Scandinavian mythology is a component of a well-organized and old indigenous religion followed mostly by Germanic peoples, a group of communities in the north and central Europe who are unified by a common language and set of religious beliefs. This religious system was most prevalent in the years leading up to the Medieval Era when Christianity overtook it as the major religion of the world.

According to Norse mythology, tales were used by worshippers to organize and comprehend the world, just as stories from any religion are being used by devotees to organize and explain the universe. The gods, who were alive, breathing deities who were a significant part of the lives of the northern Germanic peoples, are the main players in those tales.

When it comes to the Viking Age, the Norse are well-known for their exploits.

A period marked by violence and turmoil, it started in 793 CE with an assault on the Lindisfarne Monasteries in northern England and concluded in 1066 CE with both the War of Stamford Bridge in the English county of Lin-

coln. The Norse peoples, under pressure from the south from growing Christian kingdoms and headed by monarchs such as Charlemagne, fought coming empires by ravaging much of Christendom and capturing vast swaths of current France and the United Kingdom. A few of them followed the horizon to Baghdad in the United States and Northern America, sharing information with the people they encountered along the route. While the Norse were well-known for their ferocity, it was armed invasions, crafty Vikings who used Catholic beliefs to subjugate neighboring Nordic peoples, and powerful ruling families using the crucifix to cement their control that finally compelled the Norse to join Christianity.

Chapter 1

THE HISTORY OF ASATRU

Chapter 1: The History of Asatru

The Norse religions are divided into three subgroups, which are designated as Vanuatu, Asatru, and Rokkatru, respectively. During the 1960s and 1970s, these siblings grew up together. Each is centered on the devotion of a few of the 3 Norse god groups, and each has its unique style. Asatru, the eldest of the three, is principally devoted to the worship of the Aesir. Most well-known Norse deities, like Odin, Thor, and Loki are considered to be Aesir, or gods associated with human civilization, and are so included in this category. With its origins in Iceland and subsequent dissemination around the globe, the term has been more associated with the Aesir throughout time.

Diana Paxson is among the most well-known Asatru singers in the English-speaking world. In addition to Vanuatu, Asatru, and Rokkatru are modern ideologies that have emerged from Asatru. Many of their traditions are similar to those of Asatru, although they lay a distinct emphasis on them. Vanuatu places a strong emphasis on the Vanir, the spirits who are active in the ties between humans and nature. As a reaction to Asatru's Aesir-centric customs, people who believed the Vanir were devalued and were more inclined to that tribe formed the nation of Vanuatu. Vanir's gods Freyja and Freyr are two of his most famous creations. As the youngest of the three religions, Rokkatru is also known as Thursatru. It is centered on veneration for such Jötnar, the deities who are often recognized as giants and who are associated with the whole spectrum of nature's powers.

A growing number of individuals are embracing a spiritual practice based on the traditions and rituals of their Norse ancestors. Although some Norse Pagans refer to themselves as Heathens to express their principles and beliefs, the majority refer to themselves as Asatru.

History of the Asatru Movement

Asatru emerged in the 1970s as a renaissance of Germanic Paganism. The slenska satrarfélagi was established on the Summer Solstice of 1972 in Iceland and was established as an official religion the succeeding year. Shortly after, the Asatru Free Assembly was formed in the United States, although it

was later renamed the Asatru Folk Assembly. The Asatru Alliance, created by Valgard Murray, has already been holding an annual celebration called "Althing" almost for twenty-five years.

Many Asatruar, and rightfully so, prefer to use the term "Heathen" to "Neopagan." As a reconstructionist path, many of them argue that their religion is very similar in its modern form to the mythology that existed hundreds of years ago previous to the Christianization of the Norse nations. According to Lena Wolfsdottir, an Ohio Asatruar who asked to remain anonymous, "A lot of Neopagan traditions are a mix of the ancient and the modern. Asatru is a polytheistic path based on historical accounts, particularly the stories contained in the Norse Eddas, which are some of the oldest surviving records."

Beliefs of the Asatru

The gods, as per the Asatru, are living creatures who play an active part in the planet and its inhabitants. Within the Asatru system, there are three sorts of deities:

- The Aesir: Community or clan gods who symbolize sovereignty.

- The Vanir: Not directly associated with the clan, but representing soil and nature.

- The Jötnar: The giants who are constantly in conflict with the Aesir and symbolize destruction and chaos.

According to the Asatru, individuals killed in the war are taken to Valhalla by Freyja and her Valkyries. They will eat Särimner, a pig that is butchered and reincarnated each day with the Gods.

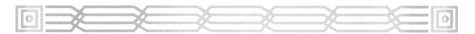

According to certain Asatruar traditions, individuals who have lived a dishonest or sinful life go to Hifhel, a region of suffering. Everyone else continues to Hel, a sanctuary of serenity and harmony.

The Nine Noble Virtues are a set of guidelines followed by modern American Asatruar. They are as follows:

1. Courage consists of both physical and moral courage.

2. There are two kinds of truth: spiritual truth and physical truth.

3. Honor is characterized as one's reputation and moral compass.

4. Fidelity means remaining devoted to the Gods, kin, a spouse, and the community.

5. Discipline is the use of one's personal will to sustain integrity and other values.

6. Hospitality entails treating others with dignity and being a part of the community.

7. Industriousness: The use of hard work to attain a goal.

8. Self-sufficiency: Caring for oneself while keeping relationships with God.

9. Perseverance is the ability to persist in the face of adversity.

Asatruar worships the Norse gods. Odin is the father figure, the one-eyed god. He is a wise man and magician who discovered the mysteries of the runes by hanging himself for nine nights on the tree Yggdrasil. Thor, his son, is the thunder god who wields the heavenly Hammer Mjölnir. Thursday (Thor's Day) is named after him.

Frey is the god of peace and abundance, bringing fertility and wealth. This Njord son was born around the Winter Solstice. Loki is a trickster deity who brings conflict and disorder into the world. He causes change by challenging the gods.

Freyja is a goddess of love, beauty, and sensuality. She is the Valkyrie's captain, and she takes warriors to Valhalla after they are killed in combat. Frigg is Odin's wife and the goddess of the household, who guards married women.

Kindreds, or local worship groups, are used by the Asatru. These are also known as garth, stead, or skeppslag. Kindreds are made up of families, people, or hearths and may or may not be associated with a national organization. Kindred members might be related via blood or marriage.

A Kindred is typically led by a Goar, a preacher, and a monarch who serves as the "holy voice."

Many Heathens and Asatruar are currently entangled in a controversy originating from white supremacist organizations' usage of Norse iconography. According to CNN's Joshua Rood, these supremacists "Satr did not give rise to movements. They arose from racial or white power movements that embraced satr, because a religion from Northern Europe is a more effective instrument to a "white nationalist" than one from elsewhere."

The vast majority of American Heathens deny any affiliation with racist organizations. Groups who identify as "Odinist" rather than Heathen or Asatru, in particular, are more committed to the concept of white racial purity. In The Role of Religion in the Collective Identity of the White Racialist Movement, Betty A. Dobratz states, "The development of racial pride is crucial in distinguishing whites who belong to this movement from whites who do not." In other words, white supremacist groups see no distinction between culture and race, whereas non-racist groups believe in adhering to their cultural ideas.

Chapter 2

THE VALUES OF NORSE PAGANISM

Chapter 2: The Values of Norse Paganism

The founding principles serve as the foundation for all other values. They are central to Radical Norse's ethical philosophy.

Underlying Values

The Underlying Values influence life's deepest truths, reality, and the fundamental ideals that guide all of humanity. Everyone else in this practice is a result of these. Autonomy, right action, and weregild are the three.

Autonomy

All sentient organisms are born with the ability to make their own decisions, design their existence, and live freely within the Nine Worlds. Every being is born free and self-governing. Autonomy also implies that it is never proper for the few to control the many, oppress others in the name of bolstering personal authority or social structures, or for anybody to rule by elevating one race, ethnicity, caste, gender, sexuality, class, or vocation above all others. This would be a violation of others' autonomy, depriving them of the most fundamental aspect of all life. This is something that neither the deities nor Fates can deny. The creation of the first humans is the best example of innate autonomy in lore. According to the Voluspa, "Three came forth from the crowd, from the home of the gods, mighty and gracious; two without fate on the ground they discovered, Ask and Embla, empty of might. They lacked soul, sense, heat, motion, and goodly hue; soul gave Odin, sense gave Hoenir, and heat gave Lodur and goodly hue."

What is most essential from an ethical sense is that the gods do not give the first humans any decrees, instructions, or laws before or after they give these gifts. All the more crucially, the gods do not decree their fate or grant luck or free will. This demonstrates that fate, luck, and free will are intrinsically a component of living, not gifts conferred or revoked by any power—they are necessary for existence. Even the Norns, who have control over life and death, cannot deny any being their autonomy.

This concept of free will contrasts with other types of mysticism, such as Biblical literalism. There is no creator of the universe in the Radical religion who gives commandments, laws, or structures that must be followed. The Powers, on the other hand, consider people as fully competent adults capable of making their respective choices in life relying on what they have granted civilization. If indeed the divine cannot create or abolish anyone's autonomy, then no one has the right to deny others' organization deliberately. Whether any group or individual is deliberately repressing the autonomy of others, whether under their authority or elsewhere in their particular demographic, whichever activities are necessary to shatter their authority and assure such atrocities never happen again.

One might extrapolate that autonomy advocates for total, unrestricted liberty for everyone to do anything anyone chooses as long as it does not impede on the sovereignty of many others. This is one aspect of autonomy, but it is not the only way to comprehend this notion. The role of society in autonomy is just as significant as the role of the individual. The fact that humans form all kinds of communities demonstrates that people cannot be fully free unless they have others to foster, guard, and sustain their autonomy. Any society in which everyone is simply concerned with oneself is governed by an everlasting battle of all against all — true autonomy is unattainable.

You're undoubtedly wondering how to ensure that all aspects of autonomy are respected. The goal is to understand and respect permission, which is the most obvious expression of personal and communal autonomy. You establish what behaviors, conditions, and coordination mechanisms you should and should not embrace in your life through permission. This means that communities and lives based on autonomy should preserve everyone's right to consent, whether granted, rejected, or revoked. Consent is breached when someone disregards the expressed preferences of others, refuses to respect the desires of community members when decisions and actions affect them, or forces consent by force, fear of force, or fraud.

Freedom of association involves the recognition of assent and sovereignty in a community setting. Individuals and groups can select whether they generally associate with specific individuals and perhaps other societies at this point. Beginning and withdrawing to cooperate with specific indivi-

duals or organizations demonstrates freedom of association. However, all organizations and individuals have the intrinsic right to associate with whomever they choose, certain justifications for doing it are more ethically justifiable than others. It is appropriate to refuse to associate with a person or group when their remarks, activities, and observed demeanor are detrimental to others. This is consistent with the significance of acts in Norse-inspired ideology.

It shouldn't be legitimate to use individual liberty to prejudice against someone else based on their ancestry, ethnic background, color, racial group, sexual preference, or aptitude. This judgment also isn't predicated on a person's or group's actions and decisions, but on characteristics of their ørlog. By hiding behind the letter, such discrimination is unjustifiable and violates the spirit of autonomy.

Right Action

If the intrinsic autonomy of all sentient creatures is the cornerstone of ethics, then Right Action seems to be how people evaluate ethical behavior. In Radical Norse Paganism, a man's personality is measured by the total of his utterances, acts, and the repercussions of his judgments by their feelings or emotions. This famous Havamal stanza beautifully summarizes the correct action: Cattle die, kinsmen die, and so does oneself, but one thing I know never dies is the fame of the dead's actions. The concept is presented succinctly, directly, and strongly here.

All of this combines the argument that a human's activities are a reflection of their personality with the concept that the memory of activities will always outlast the life of the person who performed them. Deeds, as demonstrated in this poem, do not take place in isolation from the rest of the world. When the Nine Worlds is considered as a totality, correct conduct becomes more than just doing good actions. The easiest approach to characterize the connection between Destiny and Right Action is to say, "We are our actions, and our fortunes are our own to make." It works in two ways: that everybody everywhere is the total of their acts, which include all of their statements and behavior. It tends to be associated with the fact that you choose your particular destiny in life, and fortune is the total of all the decisions you've made.

The second way it works is the idea that your activities are formed and impacted not only by your judgments, thoughts, and ambitions, but also by the decision-making, actions, and repercussions of others' actions. Everyone's fate is in their own hands. As a result, it is vital that you make the greatest appropriate decisions, live the most moral sense imaginable, and are fully aware of the consequences.

Your decisions have an impact upon others and the environment surrounding you. Evaluate the implications of your words as part of performing correctly. Words are extremely powerful because they are thought and sentiment given form. The correct words can motivate others to act, whilst the wrong people can undercut good intentions or perhaps even cause damage to others. Words, in whatever shape or channel they exist, are a separate type of action. And, like all behaviors, they must always be weighed about what is being said, how it's being delivered, and the implications of the message. This begs the question of the role of purpose in interpreting proper action. In this philosophy, the intent is demonstrated by how someone acts.

The easiest approach to convey the concept is to look at different sorts of injuries. When it comes to causing injury to oneself or somebody else, there is a distinction to be made between intentional and unintended actions. Malicious purpose has a determined, precise end goal that is shown by the deed itself. The unintentional injury also does not have a purposeful and predictable consequence. This is not to say that non-malicious injury is insignificant. It does, however, imply that any absence of harmful purpose demonstrated in such a deed must be taken into account when analyzing activities and their consequences. When put into reality, Right Action contradicts evolving cultural preconceptions.

When people are assessed with what others do and have done, there is little opportunity for shallow materialist worth based on what they own. A line from the Havamal addresses the issue of wealth directly: "I saw well-stocked folds among Fitjung's sons; now they wield the beggar's staff; wealth is as quick as a winking eye, and friends are the most deceptive." This view is confirmed further by another subsequent stanza dealing with the situation of material possessions; it demonstrates that, according to the ancients, garments do not form the person: "Washed and fed to the council food but don't be too

concerned with thine attire; no one should ever be humiliated of their shoes and hoses, let alone the steed on which they riding."

The worth of labor, which would be the total of many small and great deeds, shifts from determining how often money folks make to what kind of job they do, why they do it, how talented they are, as well as the influence their labor has had on the world. Living a life centered on Right Action places different demands on anyone and everyone than what most of current society regards as normal or commendable.

Weregild

The cornerstone of Weregild is Right Action and Autonomy. Weregild guides how to effectively mediate disputes, redress harm, and make reparations while respecting all people's innate autonomy. This concept has its roots in pre-Christian Scandinavian resolving disputes. The Scandinavian inhabitants lived in severely marginal circumstances where injury to people might endanger families and communities by depriving them of vital work. This includes making false assertions that could harm someone's reputation. Weregild was created to keep an injury from turning into a loop of vengeance and quarrels. It consisted of monetary compensation or labor offered following the damage done. If both parties agreed on the recommended Weregild, the complaint was deemed settled as soon as the compensation was delivered. If Weregild wasn't paid or even the amount was deemed insufficient, the wounded party was well within their rights to enact revenge according to their terms. This provided an incentive for everyone involved to seek out and provide genuinely fair Weregild. Transparent negotiations were used to ensure Weregild was satisfactory to all stakeholders. Weregild was introduced, discussed, and settled in front of and with the involvement of the community members. This was necessary when disagreement damaged both sides; the communities were expected to assist enforce whatever rules were agreed upon.

The purpose of almost any Weregild seemed to be to accomplish as often as possible to heal the damage done while still being steep enough to deter repeating the same conduct. Weregild is as significant today as it was during the past.

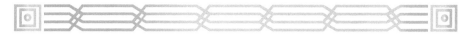

In summary, in Radical Norse Paganism, weregild's purpose is to establish an agreement in which some sort of recompense, such as material things or deeds that suit the wounded party's requirements, is legitimate throughout the eyes of the society and recognized by both parties as addressing any harm done. Whatever makes it work for reimbursement is what can be supplied appropriately, addresses the causative factors at hand, and evaluates whether the incidence is a one-time event or worthy of investigation.

It must also evaluate whether the harm was unintentional, the product of negligence, or deliberate. The disagreement should be regarded resolved though all parties consent to an acceptable conclusion as well as reimbursement has been delivered. You should not bring up a previously settled conflict even if one of the participants is repeating the behaviors and actions that generated the initial problem. That's why Weregild needs to resolve fundamental problems as thoroughly as possible rather than focusing solely on the immediate repercussions. The goal is to prevent a dispute from growing into a long-running feud of any kind by resolving the underlying causes in the most reasonable, impartial, and definitive manner feasible. However, this does not imply that Weregild must be provided or accepted for the sake of tranquility. Weregild should not be presented to anyone who might be respected to uphold its terms, and the same goes for those who fail to honor the other member on a primitive level. These activities inflict such severe injuries that neither amount of Weregild, short of absolute banishment or expulsion from a position of leadership, could ever cure the damage. It is also permissible to refuse to give or receive Weregild if another party is behaving in bad faith, regardless of whether they would have caused or allege to have incurred hurt. In general, a wounded human being deserves way too much credit unless their actions demonstrate otherwise. Although Weregild is a core ethical value, it should not be exploited to demand forgiveness for the sake of seeking forgiveness. Weregild's letter and spirit are equitable resolutions, not imposed peace based on quiet. Authentic Weregild is indeed the settlement of concerns through repayment, which solves the root problem. The awarded absolution is a result of delivering restitution and it isn't the fundamental goal.

Personal Values

If basic values lay the groundwork for morality, moral views concern the behavior of the individual. They are as follows: Boldness, wisdom, and honor. These principles serve as a guide for daily decisions and behaviors. They aid in determining what types of individual behaviors are most deserving.

Honor

If you are the total of your actions, then honor is the aggregate of your actions. Numerous researchers studying the ancients refer to their kind of honor as a public virtue, implying that it was formed on other people's impressions of you, but your activities are what make up your reputation. Your activities as a whole demonstrate your honesty. The two are in a mutually beneficial relationship. This is best summed up in one stanza, which is highly comparable to the one defining appropriate action: "Cattle perish, relatives perish. And so, one dies; however, a magnificent character will never expire; if one obtains high fame." The influence of your actions on the world is how honor develops a reputation. The repercussions of actions cause people to talk about just what you accomplished, remember it, and spread awareness about the sort of individual you are. Even actions known only to yourself influence your identity, as they modify your surroundings and conditions and leave a mark on the world. This means that you must analyze your actions in light of your present reputation, what you're doing to enhance it, and how you can keep honor. This is how honor is also synonymous with honesty. Actions that are compatible with ethical behavior are what build a desirable reputation.

Honor is much more than just wanting people to say nice things about you. It is the desire to guarantee that your behaviors are such that people would appreciate you for your good deeds. The genuinely honorable constantly adopts the much more moral dilemmas feasible, irrespective of the apparent costs and benefits. Ethical dignity would withstand misleading and deceptive claims as well as any benefits that an unworthy activity may provide. To be honorable, you must always prioritize doing good things before defending your persona or keeping up appearances. Anyone obsessed with appearances becomes a slave to their ego, committing heinous acts to protect it. If others criticize your conduct, seize this opportunity of doing yourself be-

tter progressively. If someone makes false statements, it is preferable to show them wrong by deeds instead of striking back.

Wisdom

Wisdom is a major attribute in Radical Norse Paganism and is frequently mentioned in the tradition. The following lyric summarizes how vital it was and still is: "There is no finer load to bear for wanderings wide than intelligence; it's indeed better than fortune on unfamiliar paths, and it provides a sanctuary in grief."

This prompts the question, "What exactly is wisdom?" The traditional definition is consistent with other frequently held interpretations of the notion, demonstrating that intelligence seems more than mere knowledge. Wisdom is defined as the capacity to effectively apply information. It is also obvious from the Sagas that wisdom comprises having the essential skills for collecting more knowledge, recognizing what information is accurate or wrong, and identifying which sources are trustworthy. Knowing your limits is the first step in the quest for enlightenment. This line from the Havamal explains it perfectly: "A tiny grain does have a little water, and small are all people's thoughts; however, all individuals aren't equivalent in intelligence, yet all are half-wise." Because of the immensity of all existence as well as the constraints of each person's ability to understand it, no one is entirely wise — not even the gods. These constraints should not deter you from expanding your knowledge and skills. Hiding under your boundaries (or, worse, assuming your restricted concentration or restricted variety and level of expertise is wise) is not acceptable in the Havamal: "When they sit alone in a corner, the ignorant believe they know everything; yet they never know what answer to give while others with questions arrive."

Accepting your limitations allows you to push yourself further, progress, and become smarter. Accepting the intellectual humility that comes with understanding our boundaries and the immensity of our potential is the first and most important step towards developing our abilities. Together with this prompting comes the ability to sift through a process to determine its esteem: "They will appear wise who can both query and answer properly. Nothing is hidden, as some may claim, among humanity's children." Discipline

goes hand in hand with criticism, self-awareness, and sincerity. Acknowledging how much you are capable of entails the obligation to act prudently. The following stanza emphasizes this idea: "Shun not the flow, yet swallow by proportion; Speak to the point or remain silent; from arrogance, none shall rightfully condemn him, and quickly their bed you desire."

Those genuinely enlightened need not behave rashly. They consider before acting, explain their concepts most straightforwardly and understandably possible, and are aware of their limitations, as demonstrated here: "The cautious will make moderate use of their force; they discover when among the courageous they fare that they may not be the boldest." Moderation and consistency are beneficial, yet there are occasions when pushing boundaries is vital. Finally, wisdom is much more than just having information and figures; it is the ability to evaluate their value and select the correct course of treatment in a given scenario depending on whatever you can and need to do.

Boldness

One of the most prevalent words linked with anything Norse is "bravado." Many people are drawn to the stories of heroic battles, dramatic confrontations, as well as the legacy of plundering and fighting when they first study Norse. The Sagas also glorify bravery and boldness: "The kid of a monarch should remain respectful and wise, and bold in combat as well; Courageous and happily a person shall walk, when the day of their demise comes." As demonstrated above, bravery does not imply a lack of fear; rather, it entails taking required risks, pursuing decisive answers, and doing the correct thing though it means admitting inconvenience, hazard, and controversy. The crux of this thinking is revealed in Skirnismol when Freyr's manservant, Skirnir, is questioned how he sacrifices his existence by entering Gerd's hall: "Boldness is greater than laments should be, for he whose footsteps must journey; to a predetermined day has my youth been condemned, and my life's span hereto laid."

Pushing boundaries and behaving bravely does not imply placing yourself in danger unnecessarily or putting your existence away on a whim. Stupidity is not justified by bravery. There are multiple cases whereby aggressive ingenuity is lauded. As Sigurd goes to fight the dragon Fafnir in the

Fafnismol, one great example is given. Instead of attacking the dragon noggin in a magnificent battle, Sigurdr constructed a hole, concealed in any of it, and assassinated Fafnir by striking the dragon inside the stomach with a spearhead. Throughout the legend, people who take brave action seek a definitive solution to the issue at hand. Whether it's Vili, Ve, and Odin currently rising to topple Ymir or Sigurdr slaughtering Fafnir, the decisiveness of their gestures is part of what has made them daring.

The final aspect of bravery is the issue of inaction. Without performing, irrespective of the how or even when is a deed just as much as acting. Failing to act when ethically required to do so reveals a lot regarding your personality and is harshly criticized inside this mythology, as best summarized in the following stanza from the Havamal: "The sluggard assumes they will live forever if they do not fight, but aging will not bring them the gift of tranquility, even if spears save them." It is always preferable to do the responsible thing than nothing at all. Now what the effort is and, therefore, should be is debatable, but in times of crisis, doing nothing shouldn't be an alternative. Simply because you are not personally involved in a disagreement doesn't guarantee that you will be exempted from it or that it will not affect you. In matters of ethics, you cannot remain objective. Failure to act allows immoral activities to take place.

Social Values

From fundamental and personal values, liberal attitudes are the next step outward. Generosity, solidarity, and hospitality are the three of them. These lay out how people should behave as members of a community and society. They define the ideals that should be the foundation of a community, but rather what should indeed be anticipated of everyone engaged.

Hospitality

Without the need for a question, the very well and clearly defined ethical value for the antiquity Norse peoples is hospitality. Its roots can be traced back to the difficult conditions that many ancient Scandinavian societies encountered. Anyone caught out from the public would face the wrath of the Scandinavian countryside, practically a death sentence. The practice of hospi-

tality evolved to ensure survival. Individuals in need of refuge who showed up at anyone's doorstep have been fed properly, a bed, and a secure place to stay. They were required to contribute work or presents for their hosts in exchange. These were gestures of voluntary cooperation, not simple commerce. As this verse demonstrates, the aim was compassion, not profit or personal gain: "Condemn neither thy companion nor to reveal him thy gate; come to terms very well in a person in need." Compassion for others is one cornerstone of this idea. All of those who existed in those days were subjected to and feared the situations that gave rise to hospitality. It would have been a terrible deed to turn your back on those who were suffering from such common conditions.

The following verse exemplifies hospitality's caring heart the best: "Even if it's only a hut, it's better to have a house. An individual is a virtuoso at residence; their heart is hurting, and they must beg for meals when they would rather not." Many of the Havamal verses address the specifics of friendliness, with a few of the first addressing what should be supplied to guests: "Fire is required for those who have arrived from either the freezing without with frozen knees; food and clothing are required for the pilgrim, who has arrived from the mountains." In today's world, hospitality can take various forms, from guiding and sheltering tourists to assisting people in need. Especially in the most basic meaning, how you provide or request hospitality should indeed be modified by the circumstances. Hospitality encourages you to think about how you might enhance your life or the lives of others by providing mutual support, reciprocal aid, and everything you can leave for those who are in most need.

Generosity

Generosity follows naturally from courtesy. If Hospitality is the result of sympathy and mutual aid, Generosity would be the next natural step. The practice of charity in antiquity Norse society was impacted by their way of life. They had what is now known as just presenting capitalism, in which products and commodities ranging from exquisite weapons through meals and drinks were swapped primarily on use worth rather than maximizing profits. Whenever someone had something like you needed, it was expected that you would share your wealth. As a result, the richest people in the old Scandinavian civilization were celebrated because of being charitable with

their money. The kenning "Ring Giver" was highly regarded, referring to someone who freely gave of their money to others. On a more mundane level, there are multiple instances from Havamal that encourage individuals to share their bounty with others. One passage declares unequivocally: "No huge thing need a person to contribute; often little will buy admiration; just a loaf and a half-full cup." I made a full fast for a friend. To be a giving person, you don't have to give in big, obvious ways. Although you cannot donate tangible stuff, there are other ways to give to others, including wisdom and effort. Giving was also considered as a natural aspect of companionship and the development of long-term relationships, as illustrated here: "Friends will ennoble one another weapons or robes, as each can see; gift-givers friendships are the longest found if their fortunes are fair." This Old Norse concept of Generosity contrasts sharply with the modern notion that the most admired persons are those who amass huge treasures, use their fortune to dwell in unprecedented luxury, openly indulge in various extravagance, and prioritize personal gain over other concerns.

Charitable efforts and philanthropy, while admirable, are secondary, leaving such gestures worlds apart from the ancients' generosity. Such rapacity has an unpleasant analog in folklore. In the lore, there are four convincing examples of greed being prioritized over others. This is the mighty giant Ymir, Grendel, the dragon, Fafnir, and the dragon who killed Beowulf. Though the facts of each case differ, they all have one thing in common: someone hoarding commodities or territory about themselves at the detriment of others. Their most despised trait and the source of their demise is greed.

The most obvious example is Fafnir. He was initially a gnome who, rather than sharing the money his father gave him and his sibling Reign, grabbed everything for himself. Fafnir evolved into a horrible dragon after stealing this immense wealth, and other living beings feared him. Greed turned Fafnir into a despised monster. These examples provide a lot of food for thought for modern practitioners. If indeed the ancient Romans as well as the artifacts they left behind demonstrate a different perspective of what money is for, it forces us to reevaluate how we conduct our lives as individuals and as a society. When life norms conflict with ethical behavior, you must explore different ways of behaving that are in line with such values.

Solidarity

Solidarity follows on from Kindness and Generosity. It entails standing in solidarity with others with whom you have a link, whether the bond is among relatives, society, religion, job, research, leisure, or greater aspirations.

In the lore, company, companionship, and common companionship are cherished on the pillars of shared experience. Such affinities are praised in folklore, such as those in the following passages: "I was once young and walked alone, and knew nothing of the way; fortunate know I think when I discovered a companion, for man is man's delight." Such links should be treasured, preserved, and sustained for as long as people who share them are worth defending.

As it is stated later in the Havamal, "Never be the first one to break with thy buddy the link which unites them equally; Trouble bites the heart if thy will not express to another all thy mind."

Solidarity requires all persons with such ties to join alongside, fight for a mutual purpose, and oppose those who would disrupt any element of their community. This line from the Havamal is the best articulation of this notion in the lore: "To their acquaintance a person shall prove a friend, to them now and the acquaintance of their companion; but never shall a person form a friendship for one of their foe's friends."

One of the most powerful acts of unselfish solidarity may be discovered in Beowulf, the classic Anglo-Saxon epic depicting events in Sweden and Denmark in which the hero explains why he is journeying across his homeland in Sweden towards the castle surrounded by the monster Named Grendel in nearby Denmark: "Then, unavoidably, news of Grendel gained me back home: sailors brought tales of your predicament in this fabled hall, of how it stands deserted, empty, and worthless once the twilight light buries itself beneath heaven's dome.

So that every experienced and senior councilor among my people approved my decision to travel here just to your, King Hrothgar because everyone was aware of my incredible strength."

The following statement dispels any perception that his journey was driven by greed: "Is that you won't reject me, who've already traveled far enough, the opportunity of sanitizing Heart, by my soldiers to assist me, and nobody else." Beowulf's entire purpose for coming to the rescue of Hrothgar's people is made apparent in these sections—he heard of their situation and wished to help them.

The fact that his only expressed condition was to complete the task personally with his employees rather than demanding remuneration underlines this. What makes this situation even stronger is Beowulf's point of affinity, which is about sharing humankind, among the most encompassing types of solidarity.

The Havamal expresses this thought extremely powerfully: "Whatever evil that can see evil you know, speak up against that and give your foes no peace." Friendship, mutual support, and aid are necessary for every community to operate.

This is not to say that someone who is a member of such a group should be excused from unpleasant, dishonorable, or hurtful behavior toward others. It is in this context that the instruction provided by Honor and Right Action is useful for selecting which communities are worthwhile to be a part of. More than communal history and position relative define communities. They are determined by the characteristics accepted by organization participants and how they are organized.

A Worthy Life

These ideas serve as a guide for living a fulfilling life. They are merely the beginning, as well as the intricacies of how you carry them out will differ from those of others. What is important is that you honor the essential ideals by doing your best to survive them in any way you can. Ethics, as seen above, are much more than platitudes.

They are a means of comprehension, and the Norse provides a clear road for anyone to pursue, but it is not the easiest. Every one of these morals, regardless of which aspect of life they touch, will lead you—nobody lives on

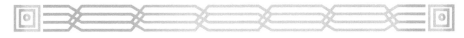

an island separate from everyone else. All acts are significant because of the impact they have on others and the planet. Every action we take has consequences that are both obvious and difficult to predict.

The following exercise will help you comprehend this better by assisting you in achieving a condition of serenity. This makes it easier to reflect on and examine your own and others' actions. It will also aid you in your activities with both the runes and seir.

Exercise: Bringing Both Sky and Sea Back to Life

This practice builds on existing training and aims to create a state of responsive calm. It is critical to underline that the purpose of this meditation is to achieve a state in which you may focus on particular goals, states, or concepts.

This meditation differs from others in that the purpose would be to integrate everything else into holistic equilibrium rather than ignoring or driving out what's apparent. Try to imagine an ocean with the sky above it once you've relaxed. Allow everything in your visualization to start moving on its own.

Don't try to make waves, wind ripples, or movement in the sky—just to let happen in the sense of feeling most natural. When you feel that it's all moving on its own, you can move on to the next part of this meditation. This portion is a little tough to grasp, so give yourself quite as much effort as necessary to get it properly.

Allow your feelings and tensions to infiltrate into very specific locations in the space you've imagined in your mind. Allow your thoughts, anxieties, and concerns to be represented as stormy weather in the sky. The more preoccupied your thoughts are, the fiercer the tempest in the skies should be.

Allow your emotions and tensions to materialize in the ocean as the heavens would become a reflection of your mind. The height, velocity, and consistency of the sea's waves and motion should correspond to your worries, concerns, and feelings.

Allow these aspects of your visualization to materialize in an uncontrolled manner. Now it is time to quiet the seas and part the storm. Feel what is driving the energies that are generating the storm. (There could be more than a root cause.) Allow the storm's reasons to affect your vision as you comprehend them. Allow the clouds to part as your thoughts clear, and the waters to calm as you gain a greater understanding of your emotions. Keep going until you get a beautiful sky, or if you choose, a bright night sky and tranquil waves.

This meditation is effective for various tasks, but it should never be viewed or utilized as a substitute for long-term treatment or other similar techniques. If you find it useful in such situations, keep in mind it was not a substitute for getting professional assistance. This practice will be difficult at first, but with repetition, it will become easier.

Chapter 3

NORSE GODS

Chapter 3: Norse Gods

There are times in everyone's lives when we have felt emotions we cannot explain. Perhaps you've experienced a spark of inspiration that solved a difficult challenge in the span of a single breath. In the aftermath of a storm's wrath, you might have felt a shiver run up your spine. Perhaps you caught a glimpse of something ancient and inexplicable out of another corner of your eye. There could have been a brief moment when you felt as if you were by yourself in the space with a powerful presence. Even more disconcerting are the times when you weren't the only one who felt the enigmatic presence. If this seems familiar, you may have previously been influenced by spirits. They are advisors, educators, guardians, formidable allies, and representations of acceptable and unacceptable behavior in the face of life's challenges for Radical Norse Paganism. They are not rulers, despite having ambitions that may drive you in unexpected directions. In the Radical heritage, they have demonstrated that they empower everyone here to regulate themselves while still offering assistance.

Understanding Divinity

There are so many gods in Norse Paganism that it is characterized as

polytheism in our understanding of divinity. Each deity is a self-contained being with its very own name, honors, character, talents, purviews, and ambitions. This is only a sliver about what the deities truly are. Even though the Norse gods, as all different religious gods, are not unlimited or even all, they are nonetheless gods. They are the Forces who lighted the stars, erected the mountain ranges, filled the oceans, and set the Universe in motion while being beholden to almost the same greater rules as just about everything in the Nine Worlds.

Understanding whatever each is called, what it is linked to, and what drives it can help understand these beings whose real forms are far beyond human knowledge. Even though the Norse gods seem powerful, yet are far from faultless. Some have scars, while some are missing limbs. The gods, like all people, have made errors and done horrendous things since a deity does something that does not make that conduct justified. The gods, in both best and worst, serve as great role models for everyone. Their flaws may appear unusual inside the face of current society's belief that divinity entails infallibility. Nevertheless, it is the imperfections of something like the Norse gods, which render their behavior, that is even more meaningful to our lives. They demonstrate that the gods confront most of the same issues that you do daily. They are supportive, seasoned teachers who want you to succeed and are not out to penalize you over mistakes or losses. They've been there and understand that taking the correct or best decision isn't always simple. The gods also are a tool for comprehending the human condition. The narratives of their acts are one way for them to set a good example for you in life.

Another way they might be identified is by what they are affiliated with. Many people now consider the environment polytheistic gods as ancient myths used to describe the natural environment leading to the rise of scientific discovery, but this couldn't be farther from the reality. Whether we're dealing with something like a deity of the depths of the ocean, a harvesting deity, or maybe one of eloquence and knowledge, the associations of a specific god allow us to understand that divinity and understand why things are the way they are. Associations give a framework for comprehending the component of life with which the god is related, and the connections also imply that the deity could provide individuals with advice whose lives are molded by such a specific field connected with that deity. The gods' influence is a different

perspective on reality; it does not reject, invalidate, or nullify scientific understanding. When used with an open mind, science and spirituality complement each other. Building long-lasting relationships are at the core of interacting with the Norse gods, just as it is in ancestor worship. This can be accomplished in a variety of ways. The following information will help you understand how each one of the deities is much like, what they have been affiliated with, and what guidance they provide. There are no certain deities that seem to be better to begin with than these; much as everyone is unique, the gods with whom you connect more naturally are the ones particularly fit to meet your requirements. Niki Ruggerio's work about relational polytheism is a wonderful place to start for ideas.

The gods of the Nine Worlds are divided into three clans in Norse Paganism: The Vanir, the Jötnar, and the Aesir. All of these tribes are related to different aspects of how humans perceive reality. The Others are gods of similar power, significance, and sway who aren't members of all the three. They do not belong to a single clan because each is linked to some of the most primal powers in existence, elevating them just above the remainder of the deities in many ways and making them a highly distinct Power.

The Aesir are the gods of humanity and civilization, with ties to language, law, labor, and conflict. They are also the most prevalent in popular culture. The Vanir are the deities associated with how humans interact with the natural environment, having links to procreation, alchemy, and interacting with nature. The Jötnar are the deities of the wildness, having a connection to raw natural elements such as wildfires, the depths of the ocean, and Earth itself.

The relationships between the three tribes and the Others are intricate. Sometimes they battle, most notably when the Vanir and Aesir waged a protracted war in the days after Midgard's birth or the numerous altercations between both the Aesir and even some of the Jötnar. They have cordial ties as well, and some have intermingled. There are no obvious, shining lines separating good from evil or light from dark between any of the three tribes and the Others. Are all simply various Powers with different impulses and affinities, and so many sides of existence.

Although the interactions between both the three families and the Others can be complicated at times, they all respect the common conventions that have been a normal part of life again for ancient Norse peoples. For example, all appreciate the sacredness of generosity, offering and receiving guest-right safeguards. Weregild, or compensation for damage and death, is frequently demanded and awarded to many members of different communities. Even though they are not always kept, vows are undertaken and respected. They all, in general, handle their disputes by open councils, debates, and popular assemblies rather than through decree. Specific conditions impact the interactions between various groupings of deities and particular deities. Although there's no overarching, cosmic battle pitting distinct tribes against one another; many of the disputes between them are the result of relatively personal, easily understood causes.

The Aesir: The Gods of Society

Some well-known Aesir, such as Odin, Thor, and Loki, may be familiar to you. Their popularity stems in part from the fact that so much knowledge about them has remained, as well as their extremely direct ties with humanity. The Aesir, as deities of all elements of society, civilization, as well as the human experience, are inextricably linked to concepts such as writing, justice, and combat.

Many Aesir are mentioned in the Sagas and many more whose names have survived to the current day, including Ullr, Bragi, Baldr, Forseti, Idunna, and many others. This chapter contains enough material to give a sense of who the Aesir have become and also to get you started on your practice. The unacknowledged Aesir are nonetheless significant in their own right, and you might just find yourself attracted to them as your practice progresses.
One feature of the Aesir that deserves its consideration is their well-known affinity for war and battle. The majority of the Aesir have such a combative characteristic, leading many others to consider they were martial deities who only embrace warrior peoples and value battle above all else. This idea seems based on a small knowledge of a classical civilization. War was a civic duty for many Norse peoples. When their villages were under attack, everybody was expected to assist in defending their homes in any way they could. It would have been more appropriate to argue that the warlike nature of the Aesir re-

flects these situations. We may deduce that almost all individuals of just about every organization have a role to play in confronting common hazards, regardless of their shape. So, contrary to common belief, the Aesir will not reject you because you are not "macho" enough—their instances demonstrate that they have entirely different priorities.

Odin: The Many-Named God

Odin, the God of Many Names, is among the Nine Worlds' most intricate deities. He has a moniker for every place he's ever been in the lore. He's also acquired a slew of additional identities, kennings, and distinctions as a result of his acts while walking the paths of reality. Despite his complexity, many people reduce him to a governing warrior patriarch with a fleeting reference of his wisdom. However, these brief glimpses of just One God barely scrape the edge of this multifaceted god. Odin is best described as a seasoned elder, world-weary traveler, and clever philosopher who saw it all, done it all, wrote the book, and then rewritten it after concluding his first try wasn't good enough.

Odin's story began after brothers Ve and Vili destroyed Ymir and built a new universe from the ruins of the old, earning the names Ygg, which means "the awful," and All-father. Following the revolt, Odin continued to test the boundaries, surrendering one among his eyes for future knowledge, stealing poetry mead, and learning seir from Freyja. His most notable accomplishment was earning the glyphs by swinging on the World Tree after nine nights and days. When he was completed, he distributed the benefits of his generosity to all the World. This act earned him the moniker "Hanged God." Odin has traversed all the Realms, learning new information no difference

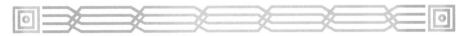

where it would be or who possessed it, garnering him the title "Wanderer." Many revere Odin as the Lord of Victory, although he usually triumphs via guile and trickery rather than fighting, frequently aided by his vast understanding of magic. Like that of the Deity of Euphoria, he is the patron of skalds (ancient and modern Norse Paganism's storytellers and poets), mystics, and savage berserker warriors.

Odin frequently appears with a wide-ranging hat ripped to shreds with one edge to conceal his damaged eye when he isn't wearing an eyepatch, as well as a well-worn traveling cloak. Gunner, the big spear, carries the authority to award conquest; all the Aesir vow their allegiance on it. He is connected to Geri, two wolves, and Freki, who consume anything thrown in front of them. Muninn and Huginn (literally Thought and Memory) are twin ravens who fly across the Nine Worlds reporting Odin all they observe. He travels through the Worlds on the back of an eight-legged horse called Sleipnir, a Loki's kid. When he is not traveling, he can be found in Asgard's hall of Hlidskjalf. There is a fantastic seat in this hall that gives whoever sits in it the ability to see anything in the Nine Realms. Odin can provide you with enormous wisdom, but only if you are willing to strive and sacrifice. His example of giving up his eyesight and hanging from the World Tree for knowledge is the one that teaches you to persevere in the face of adversity to accomplish this goal. Odin's never-ending quest for knowledge means he has valuable insights for everyone whose job includes gathering information, deciphering challenging theories, and uncovering mysteries. He provides inspiration that challenges your fundamental assumptions, thoughts, and beliefs. He offers advice on how to overcome obstacles, hardships, and struggles by looking out for unorthodox or unexpected answers. If you seek Odin's wisdom, keep in mind that nothing in the Many-Named Divine is always as it appears.

The Key-Keeper: Frigga

Frigga—Odin's wife, and partner—is as powerful as the Older Gentleman. Many people believe that because she is associated with the hearth and home, she is just a divine feminine archetype characterized by domesticity. Such assumptions neglect far deeper levels. Frigga is considered to represent some of the smartest of the Aesir due to her affiliations with secret knowledge and how to obtain it. She is frequently unappreciated in her function as god-

dess of the house, according to how society perceives domestic labor. Frigga is constantly holding a lot of wheels turning because Odin is nearly nonexistent from Asgard on his adventures and getting into trouble. This kind of outpatient labor is crucial to the survival of a community and is frequently the most critical. After all, it's pointless to battle for a spot, seek enlightenment, or create great works if neither of those actions benefits the community. Someone has to keep the power on, and Frigga is quite good at it. Frigga's hearth and house are simply the tips of the iceberg.

Frigga's well-proven wisdom, as evidenced by the Sagas, is also crucial. She does not seek knowledge passively—she has used it to modify Fates, bring favor to those she deems are worthy, deceive Odin, bring down a dictator, and endeavor to shield her child Baldr from any harm. She has constantly demonstrated mastery inside the mystical disciplines of seir. Frigga is thought to live through her chamber of Fensalir ("Fen Hall"), which is associated with marshes and all that is found inside them. Proper understanding of keys in medieval Norse society best exemplifies Frigga's multifaceted nature. Keys were an unrivaled emblem of a person's—usually a woman's—power because they offered control over entrance to restricted locations. Keys can be used to access more than simply doors, as riches, tools, records, and secrets are kept behind sturdy locks.

The ultimate key is held by Frigga, who is both the household goddess and the guardian of tremendous secrets. Her actions demonstrate that she is not frightened to use it, disclosing important information at the correct time to achieve her goals. If Odin's strategies are like those of a cunning high-stakes gambler, Frigga's are more like that of a patient chess master. Frigga brings her special insight to the table. Her strategy is to observe patiently, to work steadily, and to plan methodically.

Frigga's example serves as a model for anybody involved in work that demands these abilities, whether it's studying and researching, caring for a family, or keeping a community united. She is also closely linked to hospitality as a result of her home relationships, and she brings prudence to this realm of conduct. A weaver's distaff and a key are two of her most well-known emblems.

Thor

Midgard's Defender, Thor, is by far the most famous and well-liked of the Aesir. The Thunder God, the son of Jötun Jord and Odin, is well-known across the globe for his hammer and long red beard. He was among the most prominent Aesir in pre-Christian times, as evidenced by the ubiquity of Thorian geographical and personal names, as well as the sheer amount of Thor's hammers discovered by archaeologists. He serves as Midgard's protector against hazardous entities. Whenever his sledgehammer, Mjölnir (pronounced MYOL-neer), strikes a foe, lightning strikes, and thunder claps. Thor is frequently thought to be stupid and dim-witted, however, there are numerous instances where he exhibits incredible ingenuity and tenacity in pursuit of triumph. Only Thor was renowned as the "Friend of Man" among the gods in ancient times. Thor joyfully announces in the Harbardsljoth how he welcomes regular laborers into his chamber in Asgard, mocking more and more elite dead. His massive hammer is reminiscent of the first instrument ever produced by the human hand, as a sledgehammer is a sword and instrument that anybody, poor or rich, may possess and use.

This same Son of Earth is indeed a defender without discrimination, standing up for everyone who is in peril, regardless of where they're from or where they come from. Thor has numerous responsibilities and associations again for contemporary Norse Pagan. The first and most important position he plays is that of Defender. Thor occupies Mjölnir to protect others rather than to demonstrate dominance or might, ensuring everyone's safety and security. His associations with employees demonstrate that his protection is aimed at

ensuring people's needs rather than keeping the status quo. The Thundered moves forcefully against dangers to Midgard and its many people, just like lightning strikes with pinpoint accuracy and tremendous force.

Thor's Hammer: Mjölnir

Thor has numerous additional emblems and names in addition to Mjölnir. He is sometimes referred to as the Scarlet Deity, a color associated with bloodshed, boldness, and rage in ancient times. Tanngrisnir and Tanngnjóstr, the two goats who carry their chariot over the sky, are also identified with him.

The Harvester: Sif

Thor's bride is Sif, the deity of grain and harvest. Her most famous narrative is one in which she is the victim of one of Loki's pranks. The Deity of Mischief crept into Thor and Sif's hall and cut her hair for unexplained reasons (more probably because Loki believed it would be humorous). Loki evaded Thor's wrath by convincing dwarfs to weave her hairstyle from gold.

The act of shearing hair is sometimes seen as a resemblance to the operation of harvesting grain, linking her immediately to wheat and the yield. Sif is also considered to be among the few Aesir that has no petty squabbles with other deities, according to the Lokasenna story. It's possible to depict her merely as a goddess of fertility, yet harvesting is about more than having fertile soil. Crop production and harvesting are critical to sustaining life. It was arduous work in the early days, whenever the best instruments available were ox or horse-pulled plows, hand tools, and typically rough terrain with a limited planting season. Harvesting, in particular, was extremely dangerous labor, with injuries, maiming, and death all too often. To bring in a large sufficient yield to feed a society of any size, requires strength, commitment, and deep knowledge of the land. The power and inherent danger in harvesting add to the significance of Sif's marriage to Thor. Sif is most strongly associated with farmers and field laborers, much as she is with workers. Her rains irrigate the crops fertilized by her effort. Sif, as the deity of both crop and harvest, encompasses a wide range of characteristics. Her expertise has enormous significance for any type of task that requires outcomes. Sif's example is relevant

whether you are a teacher, an artist, a student, or active in some other project that requires long-term attention and organization. She stands in solidarity with all those who put inside the long, difficult hours that allow life to exist. She provides the knowledge of tolerance, determination, and the information required to complete the task. Sif's most well-known symbols are her blonde hair and shaved scalp, as well as the grain sheaf, sickle, and scythe.

Tyr

It is a one-handed character. Tyr, the son of Jötun Hymir and Deity of Justice, is severe but just. He embodies both the language as well as the essence of what the law is supposed to be. He is known for his strength, but he gave up some of everything for the furtherance of everybody. Many people believe Tyr stands for rigorous respect to the law; however, there is plenty about Tyr's behavior and relationships that clearly say the exact opposite. Tyr's example demonstrates the need of adhering to higher beliefs even when it requires making difficult decisions.

Tyr's most famous narrative is the one in which he surrendered his lightsaber to confine Fenrir, the Great Wolf. All other deities feared Fenrir even when he was a pup. Only Tyr was brave and sensitive enough to be concerned about him. As Fenrir intensified, his appetite rose, and many feared he would consume everyone. So, the deities devised a plan to confine the Wolf. Tyr offered a commitment to Fenrir, his de facto fostered offspring, that even if the deities effectively bound the wolf, he might hold Tyr's sword in his hand. Tyr kept his half of the bargain by allowing Fenrir to devour his hand in a single strike, creating him the one-handed deity. Regardless of his sacrifice, it helped

to avert a possible threat in more ways than one. Tyr's complicated relationship with justice begins with the story of Tyr and Fenrir. He was connected with the democratic public gatherings designated as Things (roughly tings), which served as the foundation of ancient Norse society.

These assemblies made laws, settled disputes, and elected and ousted leaders. All free citizens could speak out, submit policies, and demand justice in the Things. Lawspeakers, members of the public who held the office based on the expertise of their societies' conventions, beliefs, and norms, ruled over these areas. Tyr, as the guardian of Things, is more than just a law enforcer; he also protects the tools for truly impartial justice. He provides tremendous lessons in the present. His associations demonstrate the significance of agreement and dialogue in establishing equal social relations. He demonstrates how the letter of the law should represent higher principles and how, at times, tremendous sacrifices are required to preserve them. Tyr is however known as the Wolf's Leavings and the Oath keeper. His most common emblem is an overhand grip, which represents whatever he lost to Fenrir's jaws, as well as the rune Tiwaz.

Loki

The change-maker, Loki, is without a doubt the most infamous of the Norse gods. He is frequently vilified as an unscrupulous bringer of turmoil, and some even consider him to be a devil figure. However, probing further reveals that he is a considerably more complicated deity than a cheap Viking Satan. Loki is descended from the Jötnar, but they are Odin's pledged blood-brother and are recognized as Aesir. Loki has an important desire to bring about many vital changes, creating priceless artifacts, and taking down ancient construc-

tions. His position as a converter is demonstrated by their changeable form and deeds.

Loki's position as a change agent is consistent throughout their adventures. Such stories generally seem to follow the same pattern. Loki does something that causes an issue, usually for fun or to meet an immediate need. He solves the issues produced by his acts by winning, creating, or stealing something that strengthens and wised the Aesir. There are, nevertheless, outliers. One famous example is Loki, who insured the creation of a new defense wall for Asgard by transforming into a horse, enticing a giant's stallion, being conceived, and, as just a reward to go along with the wall's completion, giving birth to Odin's mount Sleipnir. Loki's ability to shapeshift and his uncertain gender are two of his most persistent characteristics. Loki has taken both masculinity and femininity forms at will, as well as many other forms, and doesn't appear particularly committed to any gender, rendering him a fair gender-fluid deity.

Two of Loki's most infamous moments demonstrate why some consider him to be a Norse Satan. One is in the Lokasenna Saga, where Loki interrupts a feast and criticizes all the deities for their flaws. The gods retaliated by slaying his offspring, locking him up with his offspring's entrails, and incarcerating him in a cavern until Ragnarök. Loki will lead a group of the deceased into battle when Ragnarök arrives, and their other descendants, Fenrir and Jormungandr, will wreak devastation. You could think that his actions are making him an obvious adversary of the gods, but they both follow the same constant theme as Loki's charitable acts. Loki is addressing long-standing problems and disturbing stagnant systems in each circumstance to pave the path for vital change. This is particularly the case of Ragnarök, an inescapable and unavoidable event. You don't have to agree with Loki or his tactics to recognize that his acts are almost always necessary.

In the present day, Loki is a compelling example. His malleable nature demonstrates that people may change many aspects of themselves, including those that seem to be rigid or unchangeable. It encourages you to question everything within your life and put what is in front of you to the test to determine if it is strong enough to survive on its own. Loki's wisdom is found in never dwelling on past accomplishments, accepting something solely just

for convenience or convention, and always questioning authority. This brings about change in the world, stimulates new developments, and keeps things moving. Anything that represents change or transition is also appropriate for Loki.

The Vanir: The Gods of Nature

If indeed the Aesir are the deities of civilization, then the Vanir are the deities of nature, but it is more appropriate to say that Vanir is intimately involved with how humans interact with nature. The Vanir dwells on both sides of this conflict that separates human experience from the realm beyond. Their ties to mystical activities, as well as the minority status of seir practitioners in ancient culture, reinforce their ties to borders and their ability to transcend them. Even while the Vanir are known for their magical skill and the Aesir are known for their conflict, the deities of nature are just as terrible as the wilds they cherish.

Though just three Vanir are mentioned in this book—Freyr, Freya, and Njord—there are likely many more, including those listed in Snorri Sturluson's Prose Edda. The Vanir discussed below are very well and well-revered Norse Pagans today. As gods linked with the void between humanity as well as the nature of reality, it is not unexpected that most of the Vanir have slipped through the cracks in comparison to the Aesir. The Vanir, as gods of limbo state, human relationships with the natural environment, and the more metaphysical side of things, present a different viewpoint than the Aesir. They encourage you to investigate the deeper connections that exist between you and your surroundings. Whereas the Aesir ask you to contemplate society, the Vanir ask you to consider the larger ecosystem that shapes you.

Freyr

It is known as the Bringer of Plenty. Freyr (voiced FREY-er) is a fertility god who understands the land and its natural cycles. Freyr is accompanied by hegemonic masculinity fertility, attractiveness, and potency in both ancient and modern practice. This is reflected in the numerous old bronze statues of him with a huge erect penis. He is Freyja's twin brother, the offspring of Njord, and one of the Vanir who has been taken toward the Aesir as a captive when the two tribes' war ended. He is indeed the Monarch of the Alfar, a grouping of spirits who are strongly associated with the natural world, and is known as the Bringer of Peace.

In many respects, Freyr exemplifies more loving and empathic masculinity. Freyr's courtship of his wife, the Jötun Gerd, and his final stand at Ragnarök are two of his most well-known stories. According to the Skirnismol epic, Freyr sought Gerd's permission to marry after seeing her while he sat in Odin's magical seat in Hlidskjalf, which left him completely smitten and resolved to earn her love. Freyr handed up his magical sword as part of the deal to win her over, a sword that could battle on its own without a hand to lead it or arms to swing it. Freyr deliberately surrendered an item of considerable power in quest of something he viewed as better than any magical sword, even though this choice may well have sealed his fate in Ragnarök. Freyr, along with several other deities, will ride out first towards the battlefield in the ultimate battle. He will fight the great Surtr in a violent duel on the Idavoll plain. The two will combat, but Freyr will succumb to a living inferno equipped with only an antler spear. Even when he is defeated, Freyr's legacy lives on. A greener world emerges from the remains of Surtr's blaze, much as new life emerges first from the remains of terrible wildfires. This sacrifice could be said to serve the fertility Freyr represents. He is linked with abundance and tranquility.

When starting a new endeavor, dealing with animals and plants, or nurturing new possibilities, his wisdom comes in very handy. Freyr is also highly associated with masculinity spirit, male fertility, and persons who identify as masculine. That being stated, when engaging with this part of Freyr, one must be very explicit about their aspirations. Freyr is frequently honored in annual ceremonies, particularly around the Spring and Autumn equinoxes.

His other names include the Bringer of Prosperity, the Peace-Giver, and Lord. Freyr's most frequent emblems are antlers, boars (due to his golden boar, Gullinbursti), and spring and fall plant growth.

Freyja

Freyja, the Free Spirit Freyja (pronounced FREY-yah), Freyr's twin sister, is a well-known Norse god. Freyja is sometimes portrayed as a Scandinavian Aphrodite since she is characterized as one of the most exquisite of all deities, but she is much more than that. Freyja encompasses all passions, being fiercely independent and having ties to battle and sorcery. She embodies feminine power, recognizes her desires, and always fights for her individuality. Her chariot, one of many emblems of her sovereignty, is dragged by a group of cats who work together and heed her directions.

Despite actuality, her name is derived from the term "woman." Freyja is reported to have had numerous partners, all of whom she chose, but she

lives alone and on her terms. Her famed Brisingamen necklace is claimed to have been created for her by showing the type of suitors; it is one of her most recognizable treasures. Amber also is affiliated with her because it is thought to be the result of her tears dropping to Midgard, rendering it a common gift amongst lovers. Freyja is famed for her compassion, beauty, and sensuality, yet she is also strongly associated with conflict.

Freyja receives first pick of any of the fallen brought to the gods by these powerful fighting spirits as the Queen of the Norse mythology, a troop of entities who stalk every battlefield. The remainder is subsequently taken by Odin for Valhalla. Freyja is a fearsome force in battle when employing her tremendous grasp of the magical arts. Freyja's command of something like the arts of seir, a type of Norse magic, is one of her most essential characteristics. She initially taught Odin these powers, and there are numerous instances where her abilities surpassed his, such as when she punished him for taking the Brisingamen by capturing two battalions he desired for Valhalla in an everlasting fight with her magic. This demonstration of strength was so impressive that Odin never has attempted another stunt like it since. According to legend, the Vanir's mystical strength was powerful enough to rival the more martial Aesir's force. Freyja additionally has a feathery cloak that allows her to shapeshift into hawks and falcons.

Freyja's knowledge is found in the authority you gain by standing firm with your terms. Her actions are excellent examples of personal liberty and consent. She provides advice in these areas, particularly to women and others who identify as feminine. Her deep ties to mystical practice also imply that she is frequently called upon for such work and can assist you in unraveling the mysteries of these mystic arts. Her most well-known names are Lady of the Slain, Provider, and Sea Brightener. Birds of prey, cats, the sex worker's staff, crystal, and gold are some of her most common emblems.

Njord

Knight Njord (pronounced NYORD) was a Vanir captive who was swapped with the Aesir to terminate their battle with the Vanir. Since then, he had lived with the Aesir. He's linked to the water, ocean waves, especially sailing. He lives in Noatun's hall, near the water. Despite these significant maritime linkages, Njord is not directly identified with the waters. As a result, Njord is an excellent illustration of how the Vanir represents human relationships with nature, as opposed to Jötnar's straight representation of nature itself.

Knowing Njord requires an understanding of the significance of sea navigation in ancient Scandinavia. The quickest and most dependable mode of transportation for the Norse was by ship. Mariners managed to bring in food from the sea by fishing, whaling, and hunting seals. Sailors navigated utilizing resources such as crystal shards, astrophysics, as well as the technique of dead reckoning, which relied on a sailor's extensive awareness of specific currents, tides, as well as the taste of lakes and streams. Every journey was fraught with danger, with no certainty of survival. This perilous commerce was indeed a matter of life and death for entire communities. His most well-known story is associated with yachting and sea travel.

When the Jötun Skadi traveled to Asgard seeking retribution for the Aesir's role in the loss of a parent, Thiazi, Njord was one of many men pro-

posed as a suitable husband as compensation. Skadi chose him in a blind-fold tournament where the only characteristic Skadi can see is the contenders' feet—and Njord's were the cleanest due to his proximity to the sea. Unfortunately, Njord and Skadi's partnership was not a happy one. The roaring of wolves, as well as the breeze in the trees, kept Njord up at night in Skadi's hall, and he longed the melodies of the sea. They peacefully divorced due to these issues and other fundamental differences, but there is no bad will among them. For current Norse Pagans, Njord is especially wise for those who live on or near the water, engage in nautical occupations, and whose survival depends on their ship arriving. He shares the knowledge of planning a course through challenging circumstances, persevering in the face of immense uncertainty, and discovering ways to bring crucial wealth to those in need. Njord also was known as the Giver and, therefore, is affiliated with nautical and maritime instruments, fish hooks, sailing things, and seashells.

The Jötnar: The Wilderness Tribe

If the Vanir are indeed the gods of humanity's relationship with the environment, the Jötnar represents nature in all its wrath and mystery. The Jötnar represents all that is beyond humans in every sense, being inextricably linked with primary elements including the depths of the ocean, the Earth element, as well as the ferocity of flame. Though in the contemporary world, despite all of science's and society's discoveries, there are mysteries and characteristics of the natural environment which are beyond people's influence or knowledge.

The interactions of the Aesir and Jötnar reflect humanity's relationship with nature. Although humankind as a civilization is sometimes at odds with

the environment, humans have discovered ways to coexist with the world's various ecosystems. However, where modern technology provides a degree of authority and domination, it is still stumbling due to the numerous unintended repercussions of pressing against nature's force. The Jötnar are deities of greater knowledge that exist beyond the limitations of understanding and convenience because they are Spirits that inhabit the unknown. There are several publications on the Jötnar; preserved manuscripts and folklore frequently mention numerous communities of hill fire Jötnar, Jötnar, ice Jötnar, and numerous others. The Jötnar mentioned below are well-documented in the Sagas. Many more Jötnar are likely unknown, unidentified, or are still to be met and worked with. The progenitor is Ymir.

Ymir

In Norse Paganism, Ymir is among the most significant gods. He was present at the top of all things among the first entities to arise from the combination of ice and fire. There was nothing except a huge, icy wasteland all around. Ymir survived on Audumla's milk and meat, while the cow survived by lapping lichen and moss off from the ice and stones. The first frost giants were created by Ymir, who spawned from the primordial giant's limbs, legs, and torso.

Audumla came across a bright entity stuck in the ice called Buri one day while searching for lichen. Its licking set loose this as being of light, causing the greatest shift when fire and ice clashed. Buri married an unidentified frost giant, and their son was named Bor. Bor, in return, wedded the giant Bestla, and the couple had three sons: Vili, Odin, and Ve. Even in those days, when the globe was populated by numerous frost giants and Buri's children, only Ymir could consume Audumla's milk and flesh.

There was no doubt that this directive primarily favored Ymir just to detriment of everyone else. Under these conditions, and after living under Ymir's dominance for descendants of unknown length, these three brothers would fundamentally alter everything. Vili, Odin, and Ve arose against Ymir after observing all around them how reality worked.

They slew the mighty giant, causing a flood of its blood to sweep over the world. As the flood receded, the brothers and many other gods banded together to create a new universe. They built Midgard and most of the material reality as we know it from Ymir's bones, flesh, and organs.

The narrative of Ymir's demise is important for two reasons. The first is that everything is derived from elsewhere; nothing is derived from nothing. Everything is made of materials, concepts, and inspirations from something else. Something could be acquired and molded into better versions for the present situation. The second is that, as seen in several other Sagas, Ymir exemplifies the faults of avarice, collecting, and oppressing others. Many other antagonistic entities, such as the serpent Fafnir, were bad because they hoarded wealth for themselves rather than generously sharing their bounty. Ymir's story demonstrates that current conditions can be converted into new forms and that individuals should not have to tolerate that if the existing structure is damaging to them. Existence is not a static, unchangeable entity. By taking intentional, decisive action, it can be transformed, reinterpreted, and reconstructed into new forms. Ymir preserves the mysteries of the primordial ages before Midgard for those who contemplate the enormous primordial entity. As one is to emerge through ice and fire, its wisdom is one-of-a-kind and powerful for those who seek it. Be mindful if you want to delve into the foundations of existence to communicate with a deceased giant. You might get answers you weren't expecting or prepared for.

The Walking Inferno (Surtr)

Surtr governs over the flame giants who live in Muspelheim, the country of perpetual fire and heat.

He is a gigantic, enraged being of enormous power who embodies blazing flame. Surtr bears a fiery spear that will strike the World Tree at Ragnarök's conclusion, burning all Nine Worlds.

Surtr, according to the legend, is a bearer of enormous disaster, calamity, and crisis. Surtr is easily viewed as the ultimate foe and adversary of the gods. Although there's some truth to this, nonetheless, Surtr's role is far more intricate than that of a basic foe. Surtr is a destroyer in the same manner

that Odin and his siblings were when they slaughtered Ymir, but their rise created an opportunity for Middle-earth as we understand it. Surtr, like Odin, Vili, and Ve, is an agent of change, even whether he will ultimately reign so over the realm produced by his deeds of destruction. Surtr's fire has many natural counterparts. The immense pine woods of Scandinavia rely on fire to renew themselves, whilst the World Tree does to birth new realities. Their seed-bearing cones fall regularly throughout the seasons, yet this is inadequate to produce new pine trees. This is only conceivable because of a wildfire, whether produced via natural or human causes. The sticky, combustible fluid that holds the pine needles collectively heats up and explodes during the fire, sending the seeds in all directions. The ashes from the fires fertilize the soil and make room for fresh life to bloom and flourish. Surtr's fulfillment of this greater cosmic duty does not render him ineffective or devoid of agency. As stated in the lore, his battle against the Aesir at Ragnarök stems from ancient feuds between these tribes.

Many events, such as Ymir's assassination and the deception inside the construction of Asgard's wall, inspire Surtr and his adherents to fight the Aesir and each other's companions. Surtr's role is both cosmically required and motivated by his wishes in connection to the activities of other Authorities on the World Tree.

Jord: The Living Planet

Jord is the very essence of the Earth. She is the earth underneath our feet and all that it supports. Jord is the nearest approximation to an Earth deity figure in Norse Paganism. Jord, sometimes known as Fjorgyn, is mainly remembered as Thor's mother, making Thor part Jötnar. This also demonstrates that any idea of ongoing, unrelenting hatred among Aesir and Jötnar has no validity in legend. If that was the case, Thor would have never gotten off the ground.

Jord is a powerful goddess—she is the air we inhale, the soil that yields our food, the streams that support us, and anything else that makes the whole thing possible. She is indeed the rage of volcanoes, the tremor of rumbling earth, and the fury of landslides. Whereas other deities, like Freyr, are related to how humans interact with nature, Jord represents the maternity,

home, and support required for nature to exist. Jord's intensity, width, and depth in current practice reflect nature's diversity, majesty, and ferocity. She stimulates contemplation of life's fundamental paradoxes, its dual nurturing and destructive aspects. She embodies both the beauty and peril of all that is beyond human control.

Jord's wisdom demonstrates how to address these constraints, humanity's role in the natural environment, and how completely reliant individuals are all on elements that are, at best, apathetic to human needs. Jord urges respect and humility in the face of nature's might. Her symbols include anything that represents Earth as well as the natural world, demonstrating her variety and majesty.

The Ocean Depths of Aegir and Ran

Aegir and Ran are more directly related to the ocean than Njord. People reside in a hall down beneath the ocean's depths, which also houses everyone who perishes at sea. Despite their frightening notoriety, Ran and Aegir are more than just frigid, fierce gods who rule over what is beneath the waves. They have hosted feasts for Vanir as well as Aegir in their huge hall. Aegir, also known as the Brewer, holds only one pot of water large enough to produce sufficient ales for all the divine beings.

Aegir and Ran, like the world's great oceans, can be harsh being kind and, offering and withdrawing as they want. Aegir and Ran have a lot to offer. By welcoming Vanir and Aesir in their hall, they demonstrate how hospitality is universally respected across the Nine Worlds. This relationship demonstrates that the interplay between Aesir, Vanir, and Jötnar is significantly more intricate than a simple order-versus-chaos dichotomy. The collaboration of the Aesir, Vanir, and these two gods demonstrates the need of working with the enormous forces of the wilds. The greatest emblems for them are deep water creatures such as sharks, whales, cephalopods, wave action, and other sea-related images.

A fishing net is another prominent emblem for Aegir and Ran, as it was claimed in ancient times that everyone who drowned was caught in Ran's net.

Skadi: The Icy Mountains

Skadi is among the most well-known Jötnar, thanks in part to the quantity of material about her that has survived to the present day, and also her strong connections to the Aesir. Skadi initially appears in the lore after her father, Thiazi dies. Skadi took up her swords and armor after his death at the hands of the Aesir and headed out towards Asgard to demand that the Aesir grant her vengeance for his sacrifice. The gods accepted because of the substance of her petition and her obvious martial prowess. As consolation and to encourage her to laugh, they provided her a husband. They went on to say that Skadi had no choice but to choose her partner based solely upon the feet of her possible husband. She chose the cleanest foot she saw, presumably belonged to Njord, from a line of eligible bachelors behind a screen. Unfortunately, this was a terrible marriage. Skadi adored the trees and snowfall of her mountains, whereas Njord adored the sea. Skadi was no longer at ease in his Noatun hall, where the cries of seagulls and the crash of waves interrupted her slumber. Because the two thought their problems were irreconcilable, they agreed to divorce peacefully.

Nonetheless, Skadi maintained a close relationship with Aesir after that. Skadi is associated with skiing, snowshoeing, shooting, mountains, wolves, as well as the winter season. She is also connected with sports, the vast outdoors, and the cold in current usage. Her function as one of Loki's punishers for perceived violations of etiquette even during Lokasenna also qualifies her as a goddess of retribution. Her profound knowledge can be seen in her strong, independent attitude and determination to take direct action to accomplish justice.

If you seek Skadi's advice, she would challenge you to move even while assisting you in determining your power and the best approach to attain justice. Her divorce from Njord is frequently mentioned as just an illustration of how individuals in romantic relationships may handle major disagreements graciously and part ways while staying cordial. Her most prevalent symbols include snowflakes, chunks of ice, mountains, skiing, snowshoes, and wolves, as well as hunting implements including swords, spears, and bows.

The Others: The Primal Gods

Other creatures that dwell inside the Nine Worlds exist in addition to the three tribes. They don't have a community of their own. Each one is a separate group with its background, personality, characteristics, and part to play. They represent primal energies that are much more powerful, unknown, and extensive than that of the different tribes. They provide their wisdom, which is frequently more horrible than any other. Three of these monsters are the offspring of Loki as well as the troll Angrboda, while the others are powerful beings whose origins are unknown. To study these species is to delve into some of the most profound, horrifying, and fascinating mysteries in existence.

Fate-Shapers: The Norns

The Norns are three deities that live at the World Tree's base. Their titles are Urd, which means "what is," Verdandi, which means "what is becoming," and Skuld, which means "what shall be." The origins of their names reflect the Norse concept of time, in which the past dictated what is now, the current as living in the present that is continually emerging, as well as the destiny as what will be as a direct result of previous events and present occurrences. They are the blog shapers and the World Tree tenders. They stayed just at the base of the Tree for eons, supplying water from a Well of Urdu to replenish the Yggdrasil with pristine opportunity. They imbue the World Tree with the log of the living, which further flows with Yggdrasil because it blooms and changes over time.

Some relate themselves to the Moirai of Norse mythology, the three spinners who rule over everyone's lives. This comparison has some superficial validity; after all, they determine the lengths of all beings' lives as well as how much leisure is allowed to them. The amount of control they have on the time intervening is a significant distinction.

They decide the duration of their existence and their blog, but they have no control over what happens throughout that period. Like that of the consumers of a Well of Urdr's water, they engage with the possibility in the same way that everything else does, making the best of it. Nobody knows whenever the Norns first appeared. They initially emerge in the lore shortly after Ymir's death and the formation of Midgard.

They are rarely addressed, as well as the Other of the gods automatically give them a warm welcome, never meddling with their eternal duty. Even Loki and Odin, two gods infamous for disregarding limits whenever it suits them, have never been known to seek out the three. It's indeed possible that they have power over the fates of deities.

The Norns reflect time's primeval power. They are its certainty and unavoidability. They also demonstrate how life's circumstances shape us all and how they can alter us. Their never-ending efforts to nourish the World Tree demonstrate a steady, patient determination to maintain reality intact and vibrant. Acknowledging the unpredictability of time's march and figuring out how to deal with it is the knowledge they offer. The Norns maintain everything flowing, expanding, and developing rather than freezing everything in place.

Fenrir: The Great Wolf

Fenrir is indeed the wolf offspring of Loki and Angrboda, the troll queen. The gods gave him birth and nurtured him in Asgard. Tyr has been the only god bold enough just to look for the pup because of his terrifying appearance. His appetites developed in tandem with his growth, and he was required to be more and more pleased.

The gods were frightened by Wolf's burgeoning appetite, fearing that the Wolf, whose development showed no indications of slowing or stopping, would someday devour everything within existence.

When he expanded his jaws, they extended from the earth to the farthest limits of the sky. Fearful gods conspired to restrain the wolf and save reality from his immense hunger. The gods gave three huge chains to Fenrir as a trial of his prowess, manufactured by the dwarfs one after the other. Fenrir, on the other hand, was skeptical of their motives and wanted assurances of his safety. Tyr, in return, deposited his sword hand in Fenrir's maw, pledging because if anything happened to obstruct Fenrir's freedom, the Wolf may seize Tyr's hand. The very first two strands, one made of heavy iron and one of stone, were readily broken. The final, the string Gleipnir, was made from seven objects that vanished from reality the minute the dwarfs mistook them for Gleipnir. This tie remained strong, keeping Fenrir imprisoned.

Fenrir ripped off Tyr's hand in a rage, vowed vengeance on the deities, and threatened that he would swallow Odin during Ragnarök. Agreed is the underlying factor that requires Fenrir so dangerous, as it is for other examples of deadly forces in the legend, including the serpent Fafnir of the Grendel and Volsungsaga of Beowulf.

Fenrir's insatiable desire persuaded the gods to imprison him inside the bowels of the Earth Tree. Fenrir, though, is more than just a villain. His fury and revenge exist as a result of the gods' betrayal, ensuring that he'll be a destroyer at Ragnarök. Terror was just as important in forming the Wolf as hunger was. Fenrir's captivity demonstrates the risks of allowing fear to override your better judgment, prompting you to always investigate the source of your anguish and ask if your feelings are warranted.

Fenrir's drooling is responsible for the development of the foaming stream known as Expectation, which may be seen in the world of Thor.

The river's post was in response to Ragnarök, which would be the Norse mythological event that marks the end of all kingdoms. Fenrir will release his wrath on the Gods once he has managed to release himself from the chains that have bound him for so long. Hati and Skoll are two additional uni-

que Norse mythology creatures to be on the lookout for in Norse mythology. They were both descendants of Fenrir, and they had been renowned for their penchant for running after both the moon and the sun at the same time throughout his lifetime. Hati and Skoll will eventually seize and swallow the sun and the moon, according to another popular mythology, when Ragnarök finally appears on the scene.

Jormungandr: The Serpent of Midgard

Jormungandr is Loki and Angrboda's huge serpent child, so lengthy that it circles Midgard while holding its very own tail in its jaws. Odin threw Jormungandr into the seas encircling Midgard, where it sunk, wrapped around the physical realm's bounds. It lives there, concealed and unnoticed. It reappears in mythology where Tyr, Thor, and the gigantic Hymir go fishing. Thor utilizes the head of Hymir's cow as bait to catch the greatest fish possible. Jormungandr quickly starts biting on the lure. Thor hangs on, trying to wedge in his great capture, only to see the giant snake burst from beneath the ocean. These two struggle back and forth until Hymir, inside desperation, breaks the line to prevent Thor as well as the Midgard Snake from ripping the boat in half.

The serpent will reappear at Ragnarök. Its rise from below will cause waves to drown Midgard. It will charge ahead alongside the other gods' adversaries to resolve its long-standing feud with Thor. Before Thor eventually defeats the huge snake, the two will battle inside a match that will shake the world. Despite this magnificent victory, Midgard's champion will only be ready to obtain nine steps before Jormungandr's venom overpowers him and knocks Thor out.

Jormungandr exists on the rim of known reality. It symbolizes the limitations of existence. Whatever we recognize would come crashing down as it turns against the society it once constituted, wreaking untold havoc. Some aficionados of classic nightmare literature may notice a resemblance between Jormungandr's comeback at Ragnarök and the mythical deity Mythos, another indescribable creature supposed to slumber bottom of the sea and whose rising will bring civilization to an end. However, any likeness between the two is most likely coincidental.

Hel: The Guardian of the Dead

Hel is Loki's daughter with Angrboda. Odin was so appalled by her appearance that he tossed her as far away beyond Asgard as he could, plunging her into the bowels of what would become Helheim. No other goddess or god has been as strongly identified to Helheim as well as the deceased as Hel since that time. She keeps an eye so over buried as they withdraw from the hard labor of their mortal days in this place of rest.

Hel, as caretaker of the dead, is linked to a demon of the deceased, the cemetery, and rotting. She is the inevitability of death, as well as the memories that endure despite it. If you work very closely with the deceased, you might find her to be an invaluable resource for comprehending the dead. She, therefore, offers a system of dealing with the reality of death, providing some solace that a certain part of you might live on long after your death.

Nidhoggr: The Devourer

The mighty dragon Nidhoggr lives just at bottom of the World Tree, just on the shores of a lake named Nastrond. It stays there indefinitely, preying on the dishonored dead who committed atrocities too heinous to enter Helheim, such as murdering the helpless and kin slaying. When the Corpse-Gnawer isn't devouring the very few who fall into its jaws, it nibbles relentlessly on the World Tree's roots and trunk. The dragon would never stop eating, never achieving the greatest victory in devouring its largest prey, and this is one of the few who will survive Ragnarök. Nobody knows when it first appeared.

Nidhoggr is the personification of chaos and decay. Its toil is never-ending, as everlasting as that of the tree it gobbles up. Entropy will never be satiated, just as Nidhoggr's appetite will never be fulfilled. Despite the dragon's determination, Yggdrasil survives thanks to the attention of the people who look after it. Nidhoggr's unwavering dedication to this duty, as well as his never-ending efforts to put time at bay, eloquently highlight the challenge posed by the inexorable march of time. There is no mention of surrendering to the dragon anywhere. Even the destiny that is thought to await the worst of living in Nidhoggr's belly is related to its personification of decay. Those

who perform heinous actions in life have had all but the most horrible actions eroded by time so that the only items missing from them seem to be their most terrible deeds.

The Horrible Truth About the Nameless Seeress

The Unnamed Seeress is a shadowy entity that frequently goes unnoticed in modern practice. However, in Radical Norse Mythology, she is significantly more important. She plays a central role in the lore both times she appears, delivering prophecies of Ragnarök and Baldr's death to Odin. She gives access to some of the most important truths in the lore, and what she exposes is terrifying to witness. Aside from these two unique instances, little is documented about just the Nameless Seeress. Even her name and any positions she holds are unknown. Nonetheless, these instances reveal a lot about her personality.

Odin deliberately sought her out for information in each case, stating that she had answers he can't find anyplace else. She only reveals such information after being dragged unwillingly from her mound by Odin's magic. Though this may imply that Odin has entire authority through each interaction, he is incapable to dismiss her when she begins uttering her ominous forecasts. Odin's pursuit of the Seeress implies she possessed significant oracular talents in life and death, giving her data obtained into Fate's creation surpassing all other Authorities.

The Unnamed Seeress symbolizes the most terrifying of all knowledge to modern practitioners. What she has to say is truthful and unavoidable. Her status as a deceased person who is nonetheless active and intelligent shows that her wisdom is the result of a persistent, obvious change. The Seeress' wisdom is one of confronting life's most primal realities, deepest fears, and biggest assumptions in search of deeper understanding. This emerges with the caveat that her responses may not be what they want to hear.

There are many gods but no masters. Norse Paganism's gods provide numerous paths to learning, understanding, and answers. Though this practice acknowledges many deities, irrespective of lineage, you may only wind yourself dealing with one or a handful regularly. Whichever deities that in-

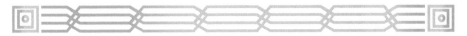

teract alongside also may fluctuate as your things evolve, you confront new obstacles and seek new answers to various problems that lie ahead. What counts is that you are continually looking for the ideal way for both you and experimenting with different views. Dealing with the gods may not be easy or simple, but the techniques that encourage you will make you stronger in the end.

Chapter 4

THE NINE REALMS OF NORSE MYTHOLOGY

Chapter 4: The Nine Realms of Norse Mythology

The universe was split into Nine Realms according to Norse cosmology. The enormous World Tree, Yggdrasil, was at the center of the universe, as well as the Nine Realms alternately extended out through the trees or existed in layers ranging from either the roots down and, barely, right and left.

The concept of síður (meaning "habit" or "custom") distinguished Norse religious doctrine, although it was fully incorporated into the life of the people. One does not attend a church ceremony, but instead worship the gods at one's own home, a meadow in the trees, or some hallowed sanctuary of mythological power. There seems to be confirmation that chapels to the gods appeared, but there is no evidence of what ceremonies or rites were done there.

The very first Nine Realms of the Norse world were most likely:

Asgard

Asgard was formerly supposed to be a part of the human realm, but Snorri placed it in the skies, linked to Midgard by Dormant, the rainbow bridge. Asgard is indeed the residence of the Aesir, and a preponderance of the Norse mythology—who fought with the Vanir, came to terms, and exchanged captives to keep that peace. As a result, while Asgard is predominantly the realm of the Aesir, Vanir lives there as Aesir does in Vanaheim. Loki, Odin, Blade, and Thor are the most well-known supreme beings of the Norse pantheon, and they live in Asgard. Asgard is shown as a supernatural city with high structures surrounded by a massive wall. It contains Odin's famed hallway of Valhalla, wherein his realm may have been housed. However, Hildskjalf, a place-name or item, is stated out of which Odin can glance out across the entire cosmos, and it is uncertain whether it is his imperial hall (distinct from Valhalla) but rather his royal seat.

Alfheim

Alfheim, which resides in the heavens near Asgard, was indeed the abode of the luminous (or shining) faeries and, following Snorri, all elves. It was held sway over by Freyr, a Vanir God who became one of the captured soldiers sent out by Vanaheim to Asgard somewhere at end of the war. The elves are magical, lovely beings that are generally influenced by music, creativity, and art.

According to scholar John Lindow (and many others), Alfheimar was the geographical location seen between banks of the waterways Gota and Glom on the boundary between Sweden and Norway, and individuals from this region were deemed "fairer" than those from other places. This region is, therefore, supposed to have inspired the fabled Alfheim, however, this assertion has been contested. The realm is not precisely depicted in Norse literature, although it is regarded to be exceedingly pleasant owing to the natural world of the elves.

Hel

Hel (also recognized as Helheim) is indeed a wicked, foreboding kingdom ruled by Hel, Loki's daughter and sister to the Midgard serpentine as well as Fenrir the wolf. Odin knew Loki's children would cause difficulty, so he placed each one where they would inflict the least amount of harm. He tossed the Midgard serpent into the oceans that surrounded the globe, bound Fenrir, and cast Hel into a dark region underneath the branches of Yggdrasil. This kingdom was bordered by a barrier only with one gateway and could be entered only by walking downhill on a long, lengthy path (called

Helveg—the way or route to Hel) and crossing a deadly river of weaponry.

For unknown reasons, her domain became connected with both the spirits of the deceased who did not die in war and, at first, those who died of illness or aging. Over time, it grew to be the most populous world of the dead, and most individuals who died were considered to journey to Hel's dark realm, where they walked in a kind of mist but otherwise continued to perform whatever they had accomplished while living. It is difficult to determine who came to Hel's domain and why, even as renowned protagonist Baldr, among many others, is claimed to have traveled to Hel when, given his stature, he should have traveled to Valhalla.

Jotunheim

Jotunheim (also known as Utgard) is the kingdom of something like the gigantic Frost Giants, located near Asgard and Midgard. Beyond the sphere of order, Jotunheim/Utgard was seen as a primordial area containing disaster, wizardry, and uncontrolled wildness. Loki, the mischievous trickster deity, was born in Jotunheim but raised in Asgard. Jotunheim was thought to be best avoided, even though there are a lot of stories about Asgard gods going there on purpose.

It must have been divided from Asgard either by stream Irving, which never went cold and also was hard to navigate, but Odin ventured to Jotunheim to Mimir's spring of wisdom, and Thor likewise went there to the giant Utgarda-stronghold. As the narrative about Thor and Utgarda, and even Loki, demonstrates that anything can occur to a person in Jotunheim—nothing Thor encounters on his voyage is just what it seems to be, and at the end of the story, the fortress and everyone in it vanishes.

Midgard

Embla and Ask, from whom all subsequent individuals descended, were the first to inhabit the human realm. Veli, Ve, and Odin are traveling along the sea after killing Ymir and creating the world when they come across two trees, an Ash as well as an Elm. They make the first man out of another Ash tree and also the first lady out of the Elm. They recognize, however, that all these creatures are defenseless and extremely vulnerable to the giants, and so they establish Midgard to safeguard them.

After creating humanity, the gods build Asgard with its lofty walls for protection, and it is assumed that they also created the creatures within Midgard and the bridge of Rainbow.

Muspelheim

According to Snorri, Muspelheim is the primeval realm of fire that played a role in the formation of the Universe. Surtr, the Fire-Giant, inhabits this world and will appear during Ragnarök, the gods' twilight, and demolish Asgard and almost everything else. Scholars today disagree with Snorri's view, believing that Muspell was initially a fiery giant whose main function in Old Norse mythology has been the role he would play during Ragnarök.

According to John Lindow, "in Eddic literature, Muspell is affiliated with organizations, Muspell's populations, and Muspell's sons." Both pertain to the legions of terrible entities who will devastate the planet during Ragnarök." Simek concurs, citing Muspell as a word for a giant that roughly translates to "the end of the world." However, as with many of the ancient Norse conceptions, Snorri's interpretation transformed how Muspell or Muspelheim had been initially perceived, and it has been considered as a place of fire, rather than a creature, for the previous few hundred years.

Nidavellir/Svartalfheim

The domain of Nidavellir/Svartalfheim lay deep in the soil beneath Midgard, and it was the habitat of the goblins who struggled there at their forges. It's a gloomy, smokey chamber illuminated only by the forge fires and lanterns on the walls. The gods appear to have determined the dwarfs' kingdom based on Snorri's account of their origins in the Gylfafinning.

The dwarfs were connected with skill and magic. They designed Thor's hammer Mjölnir, Odin's spear, and Frey's magic ship, which can be wrapped up and moved in his pocket. They are also in charge of the Mead of Poetry, whom Odin snatches from the gigantic and delivers to the gods, who would then inspire poets to compose their verse through drink.

Niflheim

Niflheim, like Muspelheim, is the eldest of the nine domains, the primordial country of mist, ice, and snow from which all life arose. Snorri associates Niflheim with Niflhel, leading to his conception of Niflheim as that of the origin of Hel's dominion. If, as appears, Niflhel existed in Norse cosmology before Christianity, there is no reference to it in Niflheim, and it was most likely a place of the dead similar to Tartarus in Greek mythology or later

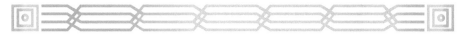

portrayals of Hel: a dark, dreary region in which the spirits of the deceased are kept. It could have been beneath Niflheim.

Niflheim, on the other hand, is irrelevant to the depths of hell in general. It is a frigid and misty land where no one, not the Frost Giants, can survive. Odin is claimed to have cast Hel into Niflheim as given her dominion over the deceased and the existence of those within the Nine Realms, and it is believed that she might have gone beyond Niflheim and then into Niflhel (which simply means "black realm of Hel"), where she would have governed.

Vanaheim

Vanaheim is the abode of the Vanir, another Norse deity family linked with fertility and sorcery. The Aesir came into conflict with the Vanir for unknown reasons. It's possible that perhaps the battle was waged over numerous Vanir customs that the Aesir found undesirable, including legalizing incest and practicing a type of magic that the Aesir felt dishonorable. Whatever the cause of the battle, it was ended by a ceasefire agreement wherein captives were swapped and the Vanir sea deity Njord with his two sons Freyr and Frejya moved to Asgard to reside.

Vanaheim is not described, although it is thought to be a productive and delightful place of wizardry and illumination. "The Vanir are fertility gods who were invoked for harvest time, sunshine, rainfall, and fair breezes, particularly by the agricultural populace, and for favorable weather conditions by mariners and fishermen," Simek adds. Freyja, amongst the most prominent Norse gods, ruled over a region of the departed named Folkvangr ("Field of the People") someplace in Asgard, which was presumably just as delightful as Vanaheim, her native world.

Chapter 5

FESTIVALS AND RITUALS

Chapter 5: Festivals and Rituals

The importance of ritual or ceremony in Pagan practice cannot be overstated, and it largely depends on the specific form of Paganism that is practiced. There are certain kinds of Paganism that include traditions only discussed with people who have progressed to a certain degree on their journey and are not revealed to others. This criterion for initiation is shared by the other arcane systems, including the mysterious religions of the Greco-Roman culture or Tibetan Buddhism esoteric practices, in that it is a prerequisite for advancement. Similar requirements may exist in Christian practice as well, such as the old injunction for "catechumens" or those who have not been christened to depart the ritual well before Eucharistic, which has been preserved in the catholic and orthodox liturgy of the church. One challenge for secretive religions is that secrecy breeds myth and Pagans are careful to stress that they do not sacrifice newborns and that they do not worship Satan, which is something that only a few of them would admit.

In this component of the secret traditions, it is especially vital to recognize and appreciate that the essence of the enigma is individually revelatory. So, the revelations will differ between individuals, but they will also differ based on the "degree" of revelation that the individual has experienced. Therefore, owing to the subjective nature of the insights received, it is not possible to divulge any of the secrets obtained.

Magic is used to explain certain aspects of Pagan ritual (which is often pronounced "magick" by those who seek to differentiate something from stage wizards who perform feats for amusement). "Magic" is a term that may imply many different things, but the easiest approach to comprehend its legal meaning is to think of it as using symbolic gestures to effect change or transformation.

Many modern Pagans emphasize the fact that the intended alteration occurs inside us, within our awareness, giving magic a spiritual or psychological connotation and significance. The existence of a force or superpowers in the creation and/or oneself that can truly enact change in objective objects such as healing is something that some people believe in. "Magic," according

to Roderick Main, is "ritual action meant to create effects without employing the acknowledged causal mechanisms of the material realm, implying a juxtaposition with scientific methods of effecting change." The application of the practitioner's will to events is emphasized in some definitions of magic. Since the time of James Fraser (at the commencement of the twentieth century), "magic" has inclined to be distinguished from religion by the concept that humans aim to control supernatural influences, even though in religious practice living beings could only gather signatures such forces for guidance. A "High Magick," occultist viewpoint is presented here, rather than a current Pagan one.

Keeping such clear differences amongst magic and spirituality and even science is becoming more difficult in today's world, given the advances in natural sciences and psychology, including in philosophical and religious thought. All three are based on the expectation of some kind of outcome and entail human interpretation. Understanding how magic works, as well as understanding how prayer works, is dependent on preceding metaphysical beliefs. Since Ronald Hutton (1999) points out, the magical practice may well be the one part of current Pagan that really can proclaim a continuity of life, as certain aspects like the usage of circles, shamanism, and shamanic ritual may be traced back to the ancients. Even if they are returned to Greco-Roman/ Egyptian conventions, pentagrams, the elements, as well as the directions of the navigation system may be filtered. From ancient Jewish and Christian magicians to current occultists, magic has been practiced throughout history.

Ritual, in whatever form it is interpreted, is a significant element of many Pagans' life. Pagans may perform rituals either alone or in groups. It may take place inside or outside to just being connected to nature, possibly at an old sacred shrine including a stone circle, or in a favorite location including a block of wood or on the coast, or in a constructed shrine including the Deity temple in Glastonbury, which is considerably less frequent.

When performed properly, the ritual may both express and develop bonds of trust among cultural and natural heritage, which may include all the saints or entities that may be recognized. The spinning of a circle, which defines the holy area and gives protection, is a common aspect. It may also be interpreted as representing eternity and equality.

Rituals often contain invitations to spirits of the place as well as to forefathers of bloodline (biological) and spirit (spiritual) descent. It is possible to designate all four elements of the compass as well as the four/five conventional components. Often, drinks and food will be shared in the group. What takes place inside the ritual might be simple or complex, structured or spontaneous, depending on the circumstances. One element that unifies many modern Pagans (except for those who practice reconstructionist traditions) is the celebration of the Wheel of the Year, which consists of eight festivals that commemorate the passage of the seasons.

Even though most of the personal festivals are antiquity Celtic/Irish in the beginnings, the existing integration of four Celtic cultural events with the two equinoxes and two solstices (events celebrated in very many polytheism and other religious faiths around the world) into the sequence of eight equally significant festivals does not appear to have been established previously than the 1950s, when Gardner put the pattern together and Nichols adopted it in 1964. (Hutton, 1999). Wiccans, druids, and goddess worshipers are all involved in the Cycle of the Year celebrations.

The Celtic New Year since Samhain, also known as "summer's end," is celebrated on October 31st and November 1st, and is considered to be a period when the curtain between the human realm and the other realm of the spirits is thin. It is the season of remembrance for the deceased. Possibly it was adapted for the Christian holidays of All Saints Day (1st November) and All Souls Day (2nd November).

It has also transformed into the current festivities of Halloween (which refers to the midnight before All Saints Day), and the distinction between Paganism, Christianity, and secular/commercial aspects is becoming more difficult to discern, as it is in many seasonal festivities. Bonfires (maybe Bonfire night is earlier than Guy Fawkes Night) are lighted to remind people of the return of the sun, and apple-bobbing may represent death and rebirth, or it may just be a pleasant folk tradition to participate in.

Yule, also known as the winter solstice (December twenty-first), is a celebration of the sun's rebirth. Candles, lights, spherical sun-shaped ornaments, and evergreen plants serve as a gentle reminder to people in the mi-

ddle of wintertime that warmth and vitality are on their way back. It seems to be a particularly natural period of the year for Christians to commemorate the birth of Christ, given the same symbolism involved in the celebration.

Imbolc, celebrated on February 1st, symbolizes the unofficial spring equinox when crocuses and early lambs emerge. Candles are lighted to enhance the effect of the growing length of days. This day also coincides with the Christian holiday of Candlemas, which honors the presentation of the baby Jesus in the chapel. This is also the time of year when the goddess Brighid, commonly known as Christian St. Bridget, is commemorated.

The Spring Festival or Ostara (March 21st), when the night and day are equal, commemorates the beginning of fresh life in the springtime, which is symbolized by spring flowers such as daffodils, eggs, and rabbits or hares, as well as the return of the sun.

This is a short period before the Christian festival of Easter, which commemorates both the resurrection of Jesus and the start of a new life. Several Pagans believed the Eostre was indeed the Anglo-Saxon deity of productivity, and also that her name has been maintained in the English version for the Christian feast of St. Oswald's. However, there is substantial disagreement over the veracity of that assertion among those who practice the Pagan religion. Beltane is celebrated on the 30th April/1st May and led to the establishment of spring and harvest. Traditionally, the selection of May Queens has been associated with the deity, and in the Roman Catholic faith, Mary is honored as the "Queen of the Month."

The Summer Solstice, also known as Litha (about 21st June), marks the beginning of the longest day of the year and is widely commemorated, most notably at Stonehenge. When it comes to the actual longest day (typically 21st or 22nd June), this event is more widely observed than it is on 24th June, which was traditionally the occasion of midsummer in ancient times and is preferred by the English Druid Order. St. John's Day (also known as John the Baptist's Day) is celebrated on June 24th in the Christian tradition. While not often celebrated in England, it is particularly significant in Scandinavian nations, when midsummer bonfires are built.

Known as the beginning of harvest, Lughnasadh (31st July/1st August), named just after the Irish deity Lugh, is celebrated with a concept of the crucifixion and resurrection of crops on the first of August. Lammas is the Christian feast that corresponds to this celebration. The Autumnal Equinox marks the beginning of the second half of the year's darkness.

MYTHOLOGICAL CREATURES IN NORSE PAGANISM

Chapter 6: Mythological Creatures in Norse Paganism

Many of these things were creatures of the night. They are spiritual creatures with a wicked appearance and a dreadful reputation that aspired to bring about disaster and bring the world of humanity to an end. However, even though nearly all the Norse mythology monsters were considerably more powerful than the Vikings, the Vikings always had the Gods on their side, whether in war or any other circumstance.

A plethora of friendly creatures was also in the Norse mythology cosmos, such as dwarfs and elves, whom the Vikings met regularly, as revealed by the Vikings themselves.

The giants, sometimes known as the "devourers," were among the most amazing animals on the planet. When it came to the mighty Aesir tribe of Gods, the chaotic entities of dark, mortality, night, and cold were often the adversaries they faced. Hel, the female ruler of the underworld, is the most well-known giant. Fenrir, on the other hand, is the most renowned character in the Norse origin tale. During the fabled Ragnarök, the wolf Fenrir devoured Odin, causing him to die.

Dwarfs

These humanoid monsters were well-known in both Viking and Germanic mythology, and their origins are unknown. Dwarfs were sometimes referred to as "dark elves" in certain circles. We think that they started as parasites from the body of Ymir, who is considered to be one of the world's earliest giants, and that they are little, twisted creatures. The great Gods of Asgard bestowed the ability to think onto the dwarfs. A tangle of foundries and mines was said to be hidden inside Svartalfheim. It is a subterranean location where the dwarfs used to reside.

Dwarfs are legendary beings from Norse mythology that made some of the world's most exquisite weapons and jewels. Several mythological items, such as the Mjölnir—the thunderbolt of Thor—and the Gungnir—the spearhead of Odin—are claimed to have been made by dwarfs.

It is said if the gnomes were stricken by sunlight, they would indeed petrify and turn to stone, according to some legends. Once upon a time, a dwarf named Alviss tried to claim the hand of Thor's daughter as his own for marriage. The dwarf was lured into chatting till the early hours of the morning when he was hit by sunlight and rendered stone.

Elves

There were two types of elves: dark dwarfs and light elves, each with their distinct personalities. Ljosalfar was referred to it as the bright elves, whilst Dokkalfar was referred to as the dark elves. Dark elves were thought to be much like dwarfs because they lived below and were black, according to legend.

The Ljosalfar, often known as the lighting elves, was indeed a sight to see. It was once believed that they were more magnificent to gaze at than the sun itself! They were regarded as that of the Gods of Vanir and Aesir, as well as one of the most beautiful creatures from Norse mythology. As the king of Alfheim, Vanir Lord Freyr was regarded as the supreme ruler of the elves.

Elves are well-known for having a conflicted relationship with human beings. They have the ability to both cure and inflict sickness at the same time. Historically, it is claimed that elves and humanity had shared a common ancestor and produced offspring that had human-like physical characteristics but also held extraordinary supernatural abilities.

Draugar

Draugar is also one of the Norse mythology beings that belong to the category of the undead in Norse mythology, and they are another member of the Draugar family. Some myths refer to them as bloodthirsty monsters (present vampires), yet they were more closely related to zombies in appearance. The Draugar creatures possessed incredible strength, and they could grow in size whenever they felt it was necessary. The odor of rotting flesh filled the air, and the sight of their decaying carcasses was a terrifying sight to witness.

To preserve the numerous things that were buried with them, including gold and silver, Draugar creatures resided inside their tombs for some time. Numerous individuals stated that Draugars were renowned to go to inhabited places and kill and consume the flesh of those who had offended them while they were alive, as well as torturing those who had harmed them during their lives.

These beings were infamous for murdering humans with their sheer power, devouring their live flesh, or even indirectly killing people by driving them mad, among other things. They became capable to invade the imaginations of the living, tormenting those who were sleeping. They usually leave a present, so that the person who has been tortured would recognize that the meeting was genuine.

It was possible to kill the Draugar by decapitating its corpse or by setting its corpse on fire, depending on the situation. If the Draugar's corpses rotted far too much, they would experience a grisly death and die as a result of the first. In ancient times, it was widely believed that a person's chances of becoming a Draugar following death were increased if they were nasty, selfish, or disliked during their existence.

Hulder (Huldra)

Hulder is a Norse mythology figure that belongs to the Ra group of beings. She is a woodland guardian, but she also guards several other locales. Incredibly beautiful and driven by seductive ambitions, Hulder is a female entity. There was bark covering their back and their hair resembled that of a cow's tail. Hulder was capable to morph itself into a beautiful girl, allowing her to mingle with the general populace. Their illusions could only be shattered if someone happened to see their tail. The reason they like to visit villages is to entice young and unmarried men into the forest, where Hulder would take them as lovers or perhaps slaves, depending on their situation. Hulder would sometimes suffocate them by sucking their vital force.

When a victim of Hulder's capture manages to escape or is set free, they will be unable to return to their captor for the rest of their lives.

Kraken

The Kraken is one of the most well-known animals from Norse mythology, and with good reason. It's an underwater monster that lives off the coasts of Greenland and Norway, and it's terrifying. They are characterized as being the size of a giant squid or octopus-like monster. According to certain legends, their skeletons were so massive that they might be mistaken for an island. If mankind were to travel to the islands, the island would collapse as immediately as they set

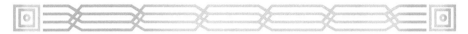

foot on it, which is how this creature was able to murder its prospective victims to feast on them. When the Kraken enters the atmosphere, it creates gigantic whirlpools that would aid in its attack on any ships in the area.

The Kraken is mostly a fish predator. It uses a variety of strategies, including expelling their intestines into the water, that attract fish due to the strong stench of their poo. Numerous schools of fish might be lured to this stench, and the Kraken would consume them all.

Ratatoskr

An animal with a squirrel-like appearance that occupies its days scurrying up or down the World Tree is yet another species from the diverse range of Norse mythological animals. The only function of this entity is to carry the instructions from the Gods to their recipients. Ratatoskr enjoys inciting conflict between the ravenous dragon that resides in the tree's roots and the wisdom eagle that resides at the summit of the tree. Ratatoskr is seen as a malicious creature since it is attempting to persuade the eagle as well as the dragon to engage in combat. The conflict with them would harm the Phylogeny due to their superpowers.

Trolls

According to Norse mythology, there were two distinct tribes of trolls. The group of them has been comprised of large, obnoxious trolls that live in mountains and woods, while the other species, known as the little-gnome trolls, live deep down in tunnels and caves and are characterized by their modest stature. The majority of the time, they are considered to be malicious and not very clever, but they have a reputation for displaying benevolence to those who ask for a favor from them. The Scandinavian landscape is littered with large stones, and it is thought that perhaps the trolls were liable for this because they utilized the boulders as weapons against the local population. Another popular legend is that these stones are trolls who have been rendered inert by exposure to sunshine.

Valkyries

Valkyries are among the most we-ll-known of Norse mythology's monsters. Their job is to transport to Valhalla all of the valiant Viking warriors who have fallen in battle. They are Odin's feminine spirits, who were noble and lovely maidens. Valhalla is renowned as Odin's celestial abode, where fallen warriors may rest in peace as they await Ragnarök's arrival.

The word "Valkyries" roughly translates as "the choosers of the fallen." Not only did the Valkyries labor for Odin, but also were the ones who were able to choose who would survive and who would die in combat. Many think that they employed their wicked magic to ensure that the result was favorable to them in this situation.

Sleipnir

"This heavenly entity was Odin's conveyance," says the legend. According to Norse mythology, Sleipnir had eight legs, and it is thought that each of Sleipnir's legs was located under one of eight different mytholo-

gical realms. According to an interesting legend, Loki is the father of Sleipnir. When Loki transformed into a horse, he got pregnant by one of the giant's stallions, and he became the father of Sleipnir.

Mare

Mares were among the most terrifying monsters in Norse mythology, and they were a source of great terror. This creature was capable of inducing nightmares in victims and sitting on their shoulders as they slept. Many people believed now that the Mare was a live soul that would leave its body, much like devils, to punish the unsuspecting at night. This concept was supported by historical evidence. Another theory holds that they were witches and that their spirits could manifest themselves as animals. It was a widely held idea that the soul may wander off during the nighttime hours. Even the All-Father Odin's spirit roamed, and it traveled so often that Odin became concerned that his soul would not be able to find a way back to his body on one occasion.

According to folklore, if the Mare comes into contact with a live thing such as a tree, cattle, or even humans, the contact will lead tree stumps or even hair to get intertwined

⅁┼⟨┼⟨

Chapter 7

The Religious Meaning of Ragnarök

Chapter 7: The Religious Meaning of Ragnarök

Ragnarök is the catastrophic fight between both the energies of chaos and the forces of discipline in Norse mythology, which ends the world and kills the majority of the deities and their foes, paving the way for the creation of a whole new world. Despite this, some scholars believe that now in pre-Christian Norse mythology, when the gods were destroyed, there was no such thing as rebirth.

Ragnarök ("Destiny of the Gods"), also known as Ragnarökkr ("Dawn of the Gods"), is the crucial event that brings the mythic cycle to a close, commencing with the parturition of the divine beings of Asgard (the Aesir) as well as the establishment of the Nine Kingdoms of Norse cosmology and ending with the death of the supreme beings of Asgard (the Aesir). To preserve the universe they have created, the deities established order and confined the powers of chaos. But during Ragnarök, these energies break the chains, although the gods are aware that they will be destined, they march to fight to rescue the civilization they have formed.

The gods fail, and the majority of them are slain, namely Thor, Odin, Heimdall, and Tyr, but the order is maintained, and a new frontier rises from the ashes of the old. Ragnarök has traditionally been interpreted—since the 13th century—like the conclusion of the Nine Realms, marked by significant climatic changes, the disintegration of old values, and the last conflict that ends the current cycle of existence and ushers in a new one. After Ragnarök, the gods who have survived return to the site wherein their town previously existed, and the last remaining mankind couple colonizes the planet to usher in a new epoch of human civilization.

There is probably a Christian impact on this interpretation of Ragnarök, and an earlier conception of the event probably resulted in utter devastation without a resurrection. Because the Norse tales were handed down orally before the arrival of Christian in the area, and because there is no historical account about how Ragnarök may well have formerly been interpreted, this assertion is called into question. In the modern-day, the occurrence is most recognized for its representation in popular culture, which includes a film, a computer game, and a television series, all of which depict resurrection after mortality.

Predicting Ragnarök

No doubt the gods will be well cognizant knowing Ragnarök, the day before the end, is approaching them. There will still be indications that it is going to happen. The assassination of Baldur is the first of these signals. One might contend that Ragnarök hasn't occurred since the world—or at the very least, the planet Earth—continues to exist. It is also possible to say that Ragnarök occurred and that the deities and titans all perished, and only mankind survived.

Baldur's death, according to those who think Ragnarök has not yet occurred, is a harbinger of Ragnarök's impending arrival. The result of his death will be a prolonged, cold winter that will endure for three years without the benefit of summertime to split it up. Fimbulwinter is the name that will be given to the winter. War will continue to ravage the earth throughout this period, and "brothers will slay brothers."

After all, if we take into consideration the Viking period, which was marked by long and difficult winters, we can see why they would believe that a three-year winter with really no summertime was feasible. If we take into account what is now occurring in the world, we may have moved beyond the assassination of Baldur and into a world plagued by conflict, where siblings destroy the lives of their siblings.

If you take into consideration assassination, violence, and gang violence, there are certainly a lot of "brothers" who are murdering their brothers.

When Ragnarök occurs, it is stated that Fjalar, a reddish rooster, would call out to the giants to warn them of the approaching danger. In Niflheim, another red rooster will sound the alarm to alert individuals who are in that realm. In addition to Gulinkambi, there is indeed a third reddish rooster that will notify Asgard of the approaching doom.

When all of the gods have been notified, Heimdall will be using his trumpet, blowing it as loudly as he reasonably can, to tell all of the Viking fighters in Valhalla to start preparing for the coming battle.

As legend has it, the conflict of all confrontations will commence, and it is stated that the Vikings who have earned the honor of awaiting in Valhalla will prepare for war. These dead, noble soldiers will don their armor and swords and fight alongside the deities against the Jotun giants, which will be their last battle. Hod and Baldur will resurrect from the grave at this point to counter one more battle with their allies in Aesir before passing away.

On Vigrid, the ultimate fight of all conflicts will take place. Going to the battlefield with his eagle helmet on and spear in hand, Odin will ride his magnificent steed to the front lines. The deities and Vikings will have made their way back to Vigrid to meet up with each other.

The Jotuns, together with Hel and her shameful death, will embark on a voyage on the ship Naglfar in the way to attain the plains of Vigrid, which will be their last destination. Fighting will also be brought to a close by the arrival of Nidhug, the dragon, who will soar above the battlefield. Nidhug is whatever you may refer to as the cleaning crew since he will consume all

of the bodies that drop on the field while still failing to satisfy his insatiable appetite.

Odin forecasts that after the mutual annihilation of any Aesir and Jotuns is complete, a new planet will be created by the gods. The planet will emerge from the ocean, lush and gorgeous as it rises green and beautiful. The Yggdrasil will be the site of the first combination of new humans—a male and a female—who will rise and seek refuge there. The moment the conflict is ended, these individuals emerge from hiding and begin to inhabit the birthing area once again.

Not many of the deities will die as a result of the battle. Vali, Honir, and Vidar are all going to make it out alive. These descendants of Odin will be present, together with Thor's sons Magni and Modi, in the hall of the gods. The sledgehammer of Mjölnir will be passed down to both of Thor's sons.

These few gods who have survived the fight will make their way towards Idavoll, the only area that has remained unaffected by the conflict. New residences will be constructed, including Gimli, which is considered to be the greatest of the best. Gimli is claimed to be a mansion with a gold-covered roof. Additionally, Okolnir and Brimir are two locales that will be formed after Ragnarök. The town of Okolnir is located in the highlands of Nidafjoll.

With good comes evil, and Nastrond is one of those things. It is a large hall that sits on a coastline that has been constructed entirely of corpses. All of the doorways in this building face north and are buffeted by horrendous howling winds. The walls are formed of twisting snakes, which release their poison into a nearby river. The river winds its way through the building. As the new nightmare or subterranean, Nastrond is just where robbers and assassins go to hide out and regroup. Nidhoggr will feast on the carcasses of these dreadful monsters after they die, according to the legend.

You may argue that Ragnarök has already occurred, that a new universe has emerged, complete with good and evil, and that the gods have chosen to stay silent rather than manifest their presence. It all depends on how one chooses to interpret the Norse myths and legends.

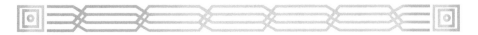

Everyday Life Affected by Ragnarök

There was a great deal of terror among the Vikings as they engaged in battle and expanded out into uncharted territory, for fear that Ragnarök would come to occur. Ragnarök was supposed to be part of the world, and only Odin seemed able to determine whether it was indeed the end of civilization or just a false ending. In the minds of those who did not trust that the Universe would survive the Great War, Ragnarök was a terrifying prospect to contemplate.

This would have had a significant impact on the life of the Vikings, who've been continuously on the lookout for the end of the world. Their faith in Valhalla and their ability to make it there, or at the very least reach Asgard and form a member of the fighting army with Freya, was essential for their success. It insured that the Vikings always live ethical and robust lives throughout their history.

Chapter 8

NORSE PAGANISM IN THE MODERN WORLD

Chapter 8: Norse Paganism in the Modern World

The documents that were left behind made it possible to learn about the Norse tales, see the collapse of the world at Ragnarök, and visit Valhalla. Epic poems and Sagas were also written by the great authors of Viking history to describe the stories of the Viking people's journeys, wars, and migration around the world. Sagas are intended to be a dramatic narrative, with stanzas of poetry interspersed to convey the stories of good men, many of whom were Vikings and renowned fighters.

The Sagas often incorporate references to both Heathen and Christian traditions to demonstrate the emergence and development of religion throughout Viking civilization. Some of the stories are romanticized and often amazing, but they also serve as a lesson in morality and ethics for the audience members. To educate people who encounter them about being courageous, battling for whatever is right, and maintaining our own culture, the Sagas are written in a poetic style.

Norse Mythology Still Exists

We cannot declare if anyone's belief is forever gone and wiped away because there are constantly remnants such as the Sagas to assist us to recollect. In the modern-day, many more are persuaded that mythological tales are a series of origin and ending of days' myths, where conflicts were conducted till the end happened.

Yet, there will still be strong believers in the customs of the ancient Vikings. Those that still believe and practice the customs of the past are mostly descendants of Viking and Germanic civilizations. They are nurtured on the legends to believe in them as Christians believed in one big deity.

For this reason, customs are still observed today. When a young lady seems to be with an infant, she or her household could light some candles and utter just a few phrases to Frigg for just a successful delivery.

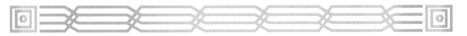

Other spiritual festivals are celebrated in a similar way Catholics commemorate Christmas and Easter. We may not perceive these festivals as religious while visiting northern European nations, but people who reside in Norway, Germany, and other Norse and German areas do. They realize this is more than a celebration to enjoy a little fun, laughs, and cuisine.

Traditions may have altered in how they will be kept, and they are also still honored via festivals, which further communicates the heritage of Greek myth with the globe. The customs of the ancient myths are still cherished and popular, which indicates they are continuously expanding. Norse mythological traditions are not developing as famous as the other customs of the globe.

It is rare to identify families who celebrate Norse customs outside of Europe. Unlike the expansion of Christianity and Buddhism, Norse customs are found in enclaves across Europe and to some degree in the United States.

Canada serves as a fantastic illustration of how many Norse customs have survived the journey over the Atlantic Ocean to the New World. It has long been speculated, and now it has been proven, that Vikings did indeed arrive in North America. It is they who first set foot on the beaches of what became Canada. Some of the most ancient civilizations on the borders of Canada continue to commemorate Norse customs to this very day.

Icelanders are extremely devoted to their Norse heritage and beliefs. In Iceland, there's been a renaissance of neo-Paganism, with the construction of the country's first temple dedicated to the Norse deities only a few years ago. Asatruarfelgio is led by Hilmar Orn Hilmarsson, who is also its founder. It is the biggest organization of people who adhere to Asatru, which would be a Norse neo-Pagan religious tradition. In January 2016, the group started construction on a new temple, which was dedicated in 2017. This is the first time this sort of temple has been produced since 1979.

That there is still a strong belief in Paganism in various regions of the globe is shown by this example. Asatru is a religion that idolizes Freya, Odin, and several other gods. They conduct weddings and burials according to the same customs that have existed since the time of the early Vikings.

Asatru adherents number around 2,400 individuals, who might adore the deities in their houses and observe many key religious events throughout the year. When compared to Christian faiths, the figure may not seem to be significant; but, in a nation with a total population of just 330,000 people, 2,400 persons who practice Pagan mythology founded on Norse mythology is a significant amount.

The Scandinavian Renaissance Fair will be taking place throughout the festivities, and you will be able to view hundreds of Swedes, Danes, and Norwegians who will be in attendance. This is a Viking marketplace, complete with souvenirs, a mock battle arena, and stories of legends. This event is growing more popular as a means to pass the time, learn about history, and take pleasure in the customs of another country, among other things.

Tourists may be there to get a good time and be amused, and for those who are hosting the event, it is about remembering a history that has played a significant role in the formation of their life today and experiencing it in its entirety.

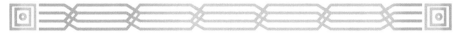

CONCLUSION

As you can see, the Norse myths have had a long-lasting impact on many European civilizations, including the Danes, Scandinavians, Swedish, and Icelanders, who are still influenced by them today.

It was the Vikings that conquered the world, and they could travel tremendous distances in their short lives. Their successors are still living today, carrying on their traditions and conducting ceremonies to spread the message about their Pagan rituals, including those of the epic battle Ragnarök, which took place thousands of years ago. Hopefully, you now understand the conception narrative as the Norse civilizations understood it, including how the Nine Realms—which may be equated to the Nine Planets in our cosmos—arose and then were inhabited by people.

The mythical creatures, along with a few of the gigantic ones who played major roles in Norse mythology, are also well-understood in our knowledge. These mythical creatures are responsible for preserving a piece of history through the customs, everyday activities, including rituals still practiced today. Sacrifices of living individuals may not be performed as often as they once were, but the belief that a tribute is essential to worship a deity has not faded.

This book should provide you with a thorough knowledge of Ragnarök, including why some people think it has already occurred and why others believe it is still in the works. Because it was supposed to have been the final destination, you have to understand it was dreaded. However, that might have been the end of civilization as we knew it, and life has improved as a result. After the course of this book, you have learned how modern traditions are based on some of the earliest traditions and how religion is continuously evolving as a whole.

Made in United States
Troutdale, OR
10/24/2023

13949251R00116